TOM SWIFT AND THE VISITOR FROM PLANET X

VICTOR APPLETON

1st WORLD
LIBRARY
Literary Society

Tom Swift and The Visitor from Planet X

Victor Appleton

© 1st World Library, 2006
PO Box 2211
Fairfield, IA 52556
www.1stworldlibrary.com
First Edition

LCCN: 2006907733

Softcover ISBN: 1-4218-2460-4
Hardcover ISBN: 1-4218-2360-8
eBook ISBN: 1-4218-2560-0

Purchase *"Tom Swift and The Visitor from Planet X"*
as a traditional bound book at:
www.1stWorldLibrary.com/purchase.asp?ISBN=1-4218-2460-4

1st World Library is a literary, educational organization
dedicated to:

- Creating a free internet library of downloadable ebooks

- Hosting writing competitions and offering book
  publishing scholarships.

Interested in more 1st World Library books?
contact: literacy@1stworldlibrary.com
Check us out at: www.1stworldlibrary.com

1st World Library Literary Society

Giving Back to the World

"If you want to work on the core problem, it's early school literacy."

- James Barksdale, former CEO of Netscape

"No skill is more crucial to the future of a child, or to a democratic and prosperous society, than literacy."

- Los Angeles Times

Literacy... means far more than learning how to read and write... The aim is to transmit... knowledge and promote social participation."

- UNESCO

"Literacy is not a luxury, it is a right and a responsibility. If our world is to meet the challenges of the twenty-first century we must harness the energy and creativity of all our citizens."

- President Bill Clinton

"Parents should be encouraged to read to their children, and teachers should be equipped with all available techniques for teaching literacy, so the varying needs and capacities of individual kids can be taken into account."

- Hugh Mackay

CONTENTS

1 THE EARTHQUAKE 7

2 THE MYSTERIOUS HITCHHIKER 15

3 REPORT FROM INTERPOL 22

4 ANOTHER TREMOR! 33

5 SECRET CACHE 41

6 BRUNGARIAN COUP 47

7 WALL OF WATER! 56

8 A SUSPECT TALKS 65

9 THE CAVE MONSTER 73

10 ENERGY FROM PLANET X 82

11 AN ELECTRICAL CHRISTENING 91

12 EXMAN TAKES ORDERS 97

13 DISASTER STRIKES 104

14 AIR-BORNE HIJACKERS 112

15 KIDNAPED! 122

16 A UNIQUE EXPERIMENT 133

17 AN URGENT WARNING 141

18 EARTHQUAKE ISLAND 150

19 A FIENDISH MACHINE 161

20 THE ROBOT SPY'S STORY 171

CHAPTER I

THE EARTHQUAKE

"Tom, we're having a problem with the gyro-stabilizer," said Mark Faber, gray-haired president of the Faber Electronics Company. "Hope you can find out what's wrong."

The eighteen-year-old inventor accepted the challenge with a smile. "I'll be glad to try, sir," he replied.

Bud Barclay, a dark-haired young flier and Tom Swift Jr.'s closest friend, chuckled. "If anyone can get the bugs out of your new invention, genius boy here will do it!"

The two boys followed Mr. Faber and his engineers to a wooden building which was tightly guarded. Inside, a secret rocket-telemetering device was mounted on its test stand.

"As you know, Tom," Mr. Faber began, "the usual conditions of rocket flight will be -"

He broke off with a gasp of astonishment as the whole building suddenly began to shake.

"Good grief!" Bud exclaimed. "This isn't part of your

testing routine, is it?"

His question was drowned out by cries of alarm and the sound of cracking glass. The walls and roof were shuddering and creaking, and the concrete floor was heaving under their feet.

"Look out! The test stand's breaking loose!" Tom warned.

Mr. Faber and two of his men tried frantically to brace the heavy test stand which held the telemetering device. Another engineer rushed toward the door to see what was happening outside. Before he reached it, another shock knocked all of them off their feet.

Electronic equipment cascaded from the wall shelves, and a heavy-duty chain hoist came loose from its overhead track, plunging to the floor with a terrifying crash.

"An earthquake!" Tom gasped.

Bud, meanwhile, clawed a handhold on a wire screen enclosing an air compressor and pulled himself to his feet. But the next moment a third, more violent tremor rocked the building, knocking him over. "The roof! It's caving in!" he heard someone scream.

As his eyes flashed upward in panic, Bud caught a brief glimpse of the ponderous test stand with the priceless telemeter tilting to one side. An instant later it crashed over, pinning Mark Faber beneath it!

Bud threw up his arms to protect himself, but too late! A falling beam caught him on the back of the head and the young flier blacked out.

For minutes, no one stirred among the wreckage. Then Tom, who had been stunned by some falling debris, raised himself to a sitting position.

"Good night!" Tom's eyes focused in horror on the wreckage enveloped by still-billowing dust.

The sky was visible through several gaping holes in the roof, which was sagging dangerously on its supporting trusses. Only two thirds of the walls were still standing.

Suddenly Tom stiffened in fear. "Bud!" The young inventor had just noticed his friend lying pinned beneath a heavy beam nearby. *Was he still breathing?*

Disregarding his own injuries, Tom hastily freed himself from the debris and groped his way to Bud's side. With a desperate heave, he shoved the beam away, then cradled Bud's head in his arm. His friend's eyelids flickered.

"Are you all right?" Tom asked fearfully.

The answer came in a groan. "O-oh!... Wow!... What hit me?"

"You got conked by a falling timber. Or grazed, at least," Tom added thankfully. "If that beam had landed square on your noggin, even a rock-head like you couldn't have survived!"

Bud managed to grin. "We grow 'em tough out in California where I come from!" he joked.

Somewhat shakily, Bud got to his feet with Tom's assistance. Both boys were heartsick as they surveyed the damaged laboratory, wondering where to begin rescue operations.

"It was a quake," Bud stated grimly. He had heard about the great San Francisco earthquake from his grandfather, and had no doubt about the nature of the tremors.

Just then Tom glimpsed a body protruding from under the wreckage of the telemetering device.

"Mr. Faber!" he gasped.

The two boys scrambled through the clutter of debris toward the spot where the test stand had been erected. Bud seized a slender, steel I beam and managed to pry up the wreckage while Tom carefully extricated Mr. Faber.

The scientist seemed to be badly injured. "We'd better not try to move him," Tom decided. "We'll get an ambulance."

Of the four other company engineers, two were now stirring and partly conscious. The boys found a first-aid cabinet and gave what help they could to them and the other two men. Then Tom taped a bandage on Bud's scalp wound.

"Let's see if we can find a telephone and call the local hospital," Tom said.

"Right!" Bud responded.

They picked their way through the wreckage and emerged on a scene of frightful destruction. The main plant building of Faber Electronics had been partially demolished by the quake. Power lines were down and an outlying storage shed was ablaze. Dazed and panic-stricken survivors were wandering around aimlessly or rushing about to assist the injured.

"Good thing the main shift of workers knocked off before this happened," Bud observed with a shudder. "There would've been a lot more casualties."

"Look!" Tom pointed to a huge crevasse. "Right where we landed our Whirling Duck!"

The boys exchanged rueful glances as they realized that the craft which had brought them to Faber Electronics - one of Tom's unique helijets - had been swallowed up in the gaping chasm.

"No use fussing about it now," Tom said. "Come on, Bud! Let's see about getting help for Mr. Faber!"

Despite the chaotic confusion, the boys managed to locate the plant superintendent - a harried, middle-aged man named Simkins - who was doing his best to restore order. Simkins, who had not been injured, informed them that electricians were rigging an emergency telephone line in order to get through to the nearby town of Harkness.

"Mr. Faber is badly injured," Tom said. "Why not send a car? It's only a few miles away, isn't it?"

"I'll send the plant nurse to him," Simkins said. "As for going to town, take a look at the parking lot." He pointed with a jerk of his thumb. The cars on the lot had been smashed into junk by bricks from a collapsing wall of one of the buildings. "And the only truck we had available was in that burning shed," the superintendent added bitterly.

"Tough break," Tom sympathized. "Anyhow, we want to help. Got a job for us?"

Simkins was only too glad to put Tom's quick mind and keen technical know-how to use. Within minutes, Tom was in charge of clearing away rubble and extricating anyone who might be trapped inside the buildings. Bud organized a fire-fighting crew to keep the blaze in the shed from spreading.

The telephone line was soon repaired and a steady stream of rescue vehicles began arriving from Harkness - fire trucks, three ambulances, and private cars driven by volunteers.

Two hours later there was nothing more Tom and Bud could do at the disaster scene and they hitched a ride into Harkness. The town had suffered some damage, though only slight compared to the destruction at the plant.

"The center of the quake was right under Faber Electronics," Tom remarked.

From a pay telephone, he called Swift Enterprises in Shopton. This was the experimental station where he and his father developed their many amazing inventions. Tom asked the operator to send a helicopter immediately to pick them up. He also called home and spoke to his sister, Sandra.

"What a relief!" Sandy gasped. "We heard a bulletin about the quake over the radio!"

"Don't worry, Sis. Tell Mother and Dad that we're okay," Tom said. "We'll be home in a jiffy - with big appetites!"

The helicopter arrived within twenty minutes at the place Tom had named. After landing at Enterprises, the boys drove to the pleasant, tree-shaded Swift home on the outskirts of town.

Mrs. Swift, a slender, petite woman, tried not to show concern when she saw the boys, bruised and disheveled. "I'm so thankful you're both safe!" she murmured.

Blond, blue-eyed Sandy, who was a year younger than Tom, had invited her friend Phyllis Newton to the house for dinner. Phyl, a pretty, dark-haired girl, was the daughter of Mr. Swift's long-time friend and business associate, "Uncle Ned" Newton. The two girls were as much upset as Tom's mother.

Tom laughed. "We're not stretcher cases," he said. "Why, one of the ambulance doctors checked us out."

Bud groaned. "Why did you have to go and spoil it?" he complained jokingly. "I was all set for Sandy's cool soothing touch on my fevered brow!"

Mr. Swift came into the living room just then and told Tom how worried Mrs. Swift and Sandy had been. "I tried to assure them that you and Bud can take care of yourselves in any crisis." He smiled guiltily as he added, "But I must admit I was more than a little concerned myself."

As Tom grinned, the resemblance between him and his father was very evident. Both had the same clean-cut features and deep-set blue eyes, although Tom Jr. was lankier and taller.

After the two boys had showered and changed their clothes, Mrs. Swift served them a delicious, hot meal. While they ate, Mr. Swift managed after some difficulty to get a call through to the Harkness Hospital. His face was grave as he hung up.

"Mark Faber is not expected to live," the elder inventor reported. "A pity. He's a great scientist."

Tom nodded unhappily. Sandy, to take her brother's mind off the disaster, said, "Dad, tell Tom and Bud about the visitor who's coming."

"A visitor?" Tom looked at his father.

"From another planet," Mr. Swift revealed.

Both boys were amazed and excited. "Wow!" Bud gasped. "Male or female? Human or animal?"

Mr. Swift's eyes twinkled. "None of those," he replied as the boys stared, mystified.

CHAPTER II

THE MYSTERIOUS HITCHHIKER

Tom and Bud were bursting with curiosity. Although the Swifts had been in radio contact with creatures from outer space for many months, this was the most exciting news yet!

On one occasion, the unknown beings had moved a small asteroid - the phantom satellite Nestria - into orbit about the earth. Later they had sent strange samples of the animal life of their planet, aboard orbiting missiles, to be studied by the Swifts. They had also helped Tom, Bud, and Mr. Swift a number of times when their lives were at stake while on daring voyages beyond the earth. What was their latest intention?

The telephone rang and Sandy went to answer it.

"For Pete's sake, Dad," Tom pleaded, "don't keep us in suspense! Who or what is this visitor?"

Mr. Swift smiled at the boys' baffled expressions. "The fact is that a message came through today that -"

He was interrupted by Sandy who had come to the door. "The phone call's for you, Dad. Long distance from Washington."

Bud groaned as Mr. Swift went off to take the call. "It's a conspiracy," Bud said. "Everyone's ganging up to keep us from finding out about that mysterious visitor!"

Tom grinned. "We lasted through an earthquake this afternoon, pal," he said consolingly. "I guess we can last through a phone call."

Inwardly Tom was as impatient as Bud about the exact nature of the message.

Several months ago, the space creatures had sent their first communication in the form of mathematical symbols carved on a black missile which had landed on the grounds of Swift Enterprises.

Tom and his father had decoded the symbols and beamed out a reply over a powerful radio transmitter. Later messages had been picked up by radio telescope and converted to appear as symbols on the oscilloscope screen.

"Sandy must know what it's all about," Bud broke in. "She's the one who first mentioned the visitor."

"Of course I know," Sandy said mysteriously. "So does Mother and so does Phyl. But don't think we're going to give it away!" she added teasingly.

Tom and Bud cajoled the two girls and Mrs. Swift for further information. But Sandy and Phyl only shook their heads, obviously enjoying the situation.

"At last we're getting back at them for the way they've neglected us!" Phyl said, her brown eyes sparkling with laughter.

"Come on, Mother!" Tom said. "Be a sport. You tell us!"

But Mrs. Swift too shook her head. "I'm sorry, Tom," she demurred gently, "but I think the girls are right. I'll say this much, though," she relented, "it will be the biggest challenge that Tom Swift Jr. and Sr. have ever faced!"

"Whew!" Bud remarked as the two boys glanced at each other. "That must mean it's *plenty* big news! It would have to be, skipper, to top all the other jobs you and your dad have taken on!"

Conquering outer space, probing the ocean's secrets, drilling to the earth's core - these were only a few of Tom Swift's many exciting exploits.

In his first adventure, Tom, in his Flying Lab, had gone to South America to fend off a gang of rebels seeking a valuable radioactive ore deposit. In his most recent challenge, Tom had defied the threats of Oriental killers determined to ferret out the secret of the Swifts' latest space research.

As the two boys silently recalled the exciting events of the past months, Mr. Swift returned to the living room.

Tom and Bud leaned forward in their chairs. "Well, boys," Mr. Swift said, "as I started to tell you, the space receiver picked up a message today from our unknown planetary friends. The message informed us that they are sending a visitor to earth - a visitor consisting of *pure energy!*"

"*Energy?*" Tom was startled. "I don't get it, Dad!"

"Frankly, I don't quite understand it myself," Tom Sr. confessed. "The message didn't explain how or in what form the energy would arrive. But, at any rate, they want us to construct some sort of container for it."

The elder scientist paused thoughtfully. "In my opinion, the energy which they speak of must be a sort of invisible brain. The symbols were rather difficult to decode, but apparently our job will be to construct a device through which the energy will be able to receive impressions of what life is like here on earth, and also to communicate its own responses to us."

Tom sat bolt upright. "Dad, this is terrific news!" he exclaimed. "If we're able to make this energy or 'brain' communicate, it may be able to tell *us* what the space people are like!"

Mr. Swift nodded, his own eyes blazing with as much excitement as Tom's were.

Bud, too, was deeply impressed but could not resist quipping, "What sort of body will you give it? How about a beautiful, superintelligent space girl for me to date?"

"Nothing doing!" Sandy retorted mischievously. "I insist on a handsome young man who'd have time to take two nice earth girls out on dates!"

"Ouch!" Bud pretended to wince. "I really left myself

wide open for that one!"

Mrs. Swift put in, "Goodness, mightn't it get out of control and be rather overpowering? Suppose it went berserk!"

"Rather an unpleasant possibility," Mr. Swift agreed, smiling wryly. "But I trust our space friends wouldn't let that happen."

Both he and Tom became thoughtful as they discussed the problem.

"The energy will arrive in two weeks," Mr. Swift added. "Unfortunately that phone call was a request that I go to Washington on urgent government business. So you may have to take over and work out a solution on your own, Tom."

It was a sobering thought to the young inventor. "You were right, Mother. This is a terrific challenge."

Soon afterward, the little gathering broke up. Bud, who had left his own convertible at the Swifts' that morning, offered to drop Phyl at her home.

Tom awoke the next morning, refreshed by a good night's sleep. After a hearty breakfast of bacon and eggs, he drove off to Enterprises in his low-slung silver sports car.

"Think I'll listen to the news," Tom thought, and switched on his dashboard radio.

A moment later the announcer's voice came over the loud-speaker. "Casualties from yesterday's disastrous earthquake now total thirty-one injured," the announcer reported. "Most of these are employees of the Faber Electronics plant and four are in critical condition. There is one note of cheer, however. At last report, Mark Faber, the brilliant president of the company, is now expected to recover." Tom gave a thankful sigh of relief.

The announcer continued, "The nearby town of Harkness was only lightly damaged, but the plant itself was almost totally demolished. No estimate of the losses has been released, but will certainly run into millions of dollars, including some highly secret defense items which were being developed at the plant. Scientists are puzzled by the severity of the quake in what had been considered a 'dead' area."

For the first time Tom, too, was struck by this curious aspect of the disaster. So far as he knew, no serious tremors had ever before been reported within hundreds of miles of the region.

He was mulling over the matter as he drove along a lonely wooded area, not far from Lake Carlopa. Suddenly his thoughts were interrupted as a man stepped out from among the trees ahead and gestured with his thumb for a ride.

"Sorry, mister," Tom reflected, "but I've had trouble with hitchhikers before!" He shook his head to let the man know that he did not intend to stop.

To the young inventor's amazement, the pedestrian deliberately stepped onto the road - squarely in the path of Tom's oncoming car!

Tom jammed on the brakes, and the silver sports car screeched to a stop. Only a quick twist of the wheel had prevented an accident!

Somewhat angrily, Tom exclaimed, "What's the big idea, mister? Don't you realize you might have been -"

"Shut up!" the stranger snarled. In an instant the man had yanked open the door and climbed in beside Tom.

"Take me inside the grounds of Swift Enterprises," he commanded in a foreign accent. "And no tricks or you will regret it!"

CHAPTER III

REPORT FROM INTERPOL

Tom, astonished, stared at the stranger.

"Who are you?" the young inventor demanded.

"Never mind who I am. Just do as I say!"

By this time Tom had recovered from his surprise and coolly sized up his enemy. The man was about thirty years old, with close-cropped black hair. Steely eyes glinted in a lean, hard-jawed face.

Tom wondered, "*Should I risk a fight? Or is he armed?*"

As if in answer, the stranger growled, "I gave you an order, my friend. Don't press your luck! Get going!"

As he spoke, the man thrust one hand deep into his coat pocket, and Tom felt something hard poke against his ribs.

The young inventor drove on, but proceeded slowly. He wanted time to think. Presently Swift Enterprises, enclosed by a high wall, came into view.

Victor Appleton

Tom's brain was working fast. At last he decided on a ruse. He would head for the main gate, get out, and use his electronic key without waiting for the guard to admit him. At the same time, he would press a secret warning bell to alert the Swift security force.

But the stranger seemed to read his thoughts. As Tom started to turn off toward the main gate, his passenger snapped, "Go to the private gate which you and your father use!"

"And if I refuse?"

Again the hard object poked into his ribs. "You will be what you call in this country a dead duck!" the stranger warned. "I will then let myself in with your key!"

Tight-lipped, Tom drove on another half mile, then turned in at the private gate. The man got out with him as Tom walked up to the gate and beamed his electronic key at the hidden mechanism. Instantly the gate swung open, then closed again automatically after the car passed through.

Tom parked in his usual spot. The stranger kept his hand in his pocket, still covering Tom but glancing around cautiously. The sprawling experimental station was a vast four-mile-square area with a cluster of gleaming modern laboratory buildings and workshops. In the distance, a tall glassed-in control tower overlooked Enterprises' long runways for jet planes.

Suddenly the stranger stiffened. A paunchy, bowlegged figure, topped by a white Texas sombrero, was coming straight toward them.

Tom's heart gave a leap of hope. The man was Chow Winkler, formerly a chuck-wagon cook and now head chef for the Swifts' expeditions.

"Hi, boss!" Chow bellowed in his foghorn voice. As usual he was wearing a gaudy cowboy shirt. "Who's the new buckaroo?" the cook added, squinting at the stranger with open but friendly curiosity.

"Why - actually I don't know his name yet, but he's looking for a job," Tom replied. Turning to the stranger, he added, "What *is* your name, mister?"

The stranger glared from Tom to Chow, as if not certain what to answer.

Chow's eyes narrowed. He had detected something strange in the way Tom addressed the fellow as "mister," and had also noticed how the man kept one hand hidden in his pocket. Looking to Tom for a lead, Chow suddenly noticed the young inventor make a quick "thumbs down" gesture.

"My name is..." The man's voice fell to a mumble, obscuring the syllables. "Frankly I am not yet sure I desire a job here, but being an engineer, I thought perhaps -"

The man's gaze switched back to Tom, and in that instant Chow jumped the intruder. With surprising agility for his rotund bulk, the cook bore down on him and let fly a gnarled fist at the stranger's jaw. Tom followed up like lightning, grabbing the man's wrist and yanking his hand out of his pocket.

He was clutching a snub-nosed automatic. Tom twisted

Victor Appleton

it from his grasp as the man landed, writhing on the hard ground. Chow quickly pinned his other arm and drove a knee into the man's solar plexus.

"Jest lie quiet now, you varmint, or you may git yourself roughed up a bit," Chow warned, then added, "Who is he, Tom?"

"Search me. He stopped my car on the road and forced me to drive him in through the private gate. Boy, was I ever glad to see you, old-timer!"

Tom emptied out the clip of shells. Then he searched the stranger while Chow continued holding him down. The man carried no wallet, papers, or other means of identification.

"Brand my tumbleweed salad," Chow grumbled, "he sure wasn't takin' no chances on people findin' out who he is! Which proves he's some sort o' crooked cowpoke! Honest ones ain't afeared o' showin' their own brand!"

The man muttered something angrily in a foreign tongue. Chow merely pressed down harder with his knee. "What'll we do with him, boss?"

"Let him up, Chow," Tom said. "Security should be here any second."

Even as he spoke, Tom glimpsed a jeep speeding toward them in the distance. The young inventor knew what had happened. Since the stranger did not have the special electronic wrist amulet worn by all Swift employees, his presence had automatically shown up on the master radarscope. A security squad was coming to investigate.

As Chow released the man, he got to his feet slowly. Then, without warning, he suddenly butted the cook square in the stomach. Chow was knocked sprawling!

Before Tom could counter the surprise attack, the man's fist cracked against his cheekbone. Tom, though stunned, lashed out. More punches flew back and forth. Tom landed a stinging blow to his opponent's midriff, then took a punishing one himself.

Suddenly Tom felt the stranger's hand clawing at his pocket for the key to the gate. With all his wiry strength, Tom locked his arms around the man and wrestled him to the ground.

The stranger fought like a tiger. But a second later a jeep screeched to a stop. Three security guards, led by stocky Phil Radnor, leaped out. Within moments they had the man subdued.

Tom quickly briefed the security men on what had happened.

"All right, mister, start talking!" snapped Radnor, head security police officer.

The man's only reply was a scowl of rage.

"Okay, take him away till he cools off," Tom ordered.

Disheveled and still panting, the man was bundled into the jeep and driven off to the security building.

Tom arrived there by motor scooter several minutes

later. Harlan Ames, the slim, dark-haired security chief of Enterprises, had taken charge of the case, and the prisoner was now being fingerprinted and photographed.

"Any leads?" Tom inquired.

Ames shook his head. "He won't talk and we've nothing on him in our files. His clothes have no tags or laundry marks, but I'd say they're of foreign make."

Tom nodded. "He's definitely foreign. He spoke with an accent and he also muttered something at Chow - I didn't catch it, but it certainly wasn't in English."

Ames frowned. "I don't like the looks of this, skipper. He may be a spy."

"Have you notified the police?" Tom asked.

"Right. Also the FBI. They're on the way right now to pick him up. Maybe they'll be able to worm something out of him."

Tom spent the morning in routine work in the big double office which he shared with his father in Enterprises' main building. It was equipped with huge twin modern desks, deep-pile carpeting, and roomy leather chairs.

Each of the two inventors had his own drawing board, designed to swing out from the wall at the press of a button. Small scale models of some of their most famous inventions were also placed about the office, including a red-and-silver replica of Tom's first rocket ship, the *Star Spear*; a blue plastic model of the jetmarine in which he had fought a band of undersea pirates; and also a gleaming silvery model of Tom's latest, unique space craft, the *Cosmic Sailer*.

Because of his father's absence in Washington, the burden of administering the vast experimental station now fell on Tom's youthful shoulders. Telephone calls, letters, and other detailed work occupied him until noon.

Chow broke in, bringing a lunch tray with milk, a hot chicken sandwich, and a chocolate eclair. Tom ate hungrily.

"Kind o' peps up the ole supercharger, eh?" said Chow, lingering to chat.

"Sure does," Tom agreed.

"Wal, jest remember that, an' don't go missin' any meals - or sleep, either," Chow advised as he gathered up the tray. "A brainy young hombre like you needs plenty o' rest an' vitamins to keep from burnin' himself out."

"I'll remember." Tom grinned affectionately as the leathery-faced old Texan took his leave. The Swifts had first met Chow when they were on an atomic research expedition in the Southwest. Chow had become so attached to Tom that he had returned to Shopton with the Swifts as a permanent employee.

Soon after Chow left the office, the telephone rang. Tom took the call and had just finished talking with Harlan Ames when Bud came strolling in.

"Any more news on that nut who jumped you this morning?" the young flier asked. "Ames told me about it."

"Not yet, but there may be soon," Tom said. "Harlan just phoned and said he'd had a call from Washington, asking us to stand by the videophone at one-thirty sharp."

Ames arrived in person shortly before the scheduled time. Moments later, a red signal flashed on the control board of the Swifts' private TV network. Tom flicked on the videophone and two men appeared on the screen.

One was Blake, the Swifts' Washington, D.C., telecaster. He introduced the other man, a calm-faced, balding individual in a dark suit.

"This is John Thurston of the Central Intelligence Agency, Tom," Blake said. "He thought it might be better to discuss this with you face to face."

Tom, Bud, and Ames were also visible to the pair in Washington.

"Glad to know you, sir," Tom said, and introduced his companions.

"We've identified the man you captured this morning," Thurston began. "He's in the United States on a French passport under the name of Jacques Renard. But we've just learned from the International Police Organization that he's actually a Brungarian. His name is Samson Narko."

Tom and Ames exchanged startled glances. In the past, certain Brungarian factions had been responsible for some of the most fiendish plots ever perpetrated against the Swifts.

"Unfortunately, that's not all," Thurston went on. "Interpol believes that Narko is also a member of the same rebel outfit with whom you've had trouble before."

Tom was dismayed by the news. "I sure thought that group had been smashed!" he said. Soon after Tom had balked their attempts to seize the satellite Nestria, the rebel ringleaders had reportedly been arrested and tried for treason.

"It now appears," Thurston explained, "that only one segment was quelled. Other members of the antigovernment movement are active again and are said to be strongly organized."

The CIA man related even more sinister news. It was suspected that a larger nation - by aiding the rebels - was planning a coup to take over Brungaria. They had already subverted various government agencies and were sending their own professors to staff the Brungarian technical schools. It was all part of their insidious fifth-column pattern.

"Many top Brungarian officials have joined the plotters," Thurston added, "and it's now becoming very difficult for anyone to enter or leave the country."

Ames asked for information on any rebel sympathizers known to be in the United States. Thurston was able to tell him very little.

"We keep strict tabs, of course, on all Brungarians entering this country," Thurston explained. "But even though we screen them carefully, a rebel agent like Narko may slip in - usually on a stolen or faked passport."

When the telecast ended, Tom, Bud, and Ames discussed the news grimly.

"What if Narko has pals working with him?" Bud conjectured.

"If he does," Tom said, "they may try carrying through Narko's mission."

"I'll station extra guards around the outer wall on twenty-four-hour alert," Ames promised.

Tom approved this measure wholeheartedly, but the purpose of Narko's secret mission remained a mystery. Why had he tried to force his way into Enterprises? What was he after? There was little hope of resolving these questions, since United States Intelligence had learned of the rebel movement itself only within the past few days. Thurston had asked Tom and his companions to treat the information as confidential.

"I'd better get back to work," Tom decided after Bud and Ames had left his office. Tom sat down at his drawing board and began to sketch out some rough ideas for a vehicle to house the "brain energy" from space.

Tom wondered if the brain would be able to perform actions by itself, given the proper mechanical output devices. Or would he have to help it function via an electronic computer to digest incoming information or stimuli and then to respond through servo controls?

The problem was so baffling and complex that Tom became completely oblivious to the passage of time. He sketched out plan after plan, only to crumple and discard each one.

Suddenly a disturbing thought jarred the young inventor out of his concentration. Perhaps the Brungarian rebel scientists had now figured out how to decode the radio messages from the Swifts' space friends!

If so, when the brain energy was launched toward earth, they might try to divert it to their own receiving setup!

CHAPTER IV

ANOTHER TREMOR!

Tom was appalled at this new danger. Shoving his drawing board back into its wall slot, the young inventor hurried to his desk and made a number of telephone calls.

Within minutes, a group of five of his most trusted associates had assembled in Tom's office. First to arrive were Bud Barclay, Ames, and George Dilling, the Swifts' communications chief. They were joined moments later by Hank Sterling, the square-jawed chief engineer and trouble shooter of Enterprises, and Arvid Hanson.

Hanson, a hulking six-footer, made all the delicate scale models of Tom Jr.'s and Tom Sr.'s inventions. He was not only an expert craftsman, but, like all the Swifts' key men, a trained aircraft and space pilot as well.

"What's up, skipper?" Bud asked.

"I guess you might call this a council of war," Tom replied.

He divulged his fears that Brungarian scientists might

hijack the brain energy to be sent from Planet X, home of the Swifts' unknown space friends.

"Bud, you recall Mother's remark last night about the danger that this energy may prove overwhelmingly powerful," Tom went on. "Well, just suppose that our Brungarian pals fit it out in robot form, then turn it loose against us or our friends in other countries."

Bud gave an awed whistle. "Boy, a thing like that might make even a powerful missile look like a toy!"

Even if the brain energy proved too small to be harnessed for destructive purposes, Tom went on, it might turn out to possess superintelligence. Gifted with all the scientific know-how of the space people, it might be made to reveal those secrets to the Brungarians.

"They might learn from it how to construct weapons or space craft powerful enough to conquer the free world!" Tom ended.

His listeners were grim-faced at the thought.

"I'd say that's a far worse danger than any chance of their coming up with a robot monster," Ames said.

"Ditto!" Hanson agreed.

"I think so too," Tom replied. "In any case, it's up to us to make sure the Brungarians don't switch that energy off course before it lands here."

"Think their scientists are capable of such a stunt?" George Dilling inquired.

Tom shrugged. "They're certainly far advanced in the fields of rocket guidance and telemetry. But actually we just don't know."

Hank Sterling glanced hopefully at the young inventor. "Got any ideas, skipper?" he asked.

Tom drummed a pencil on the table thoughtfully before replying. "Maybe our best bet is first to find out all we can about the lines of research on which they're concentrating. That might be the tip-off."

After a thorough discussion, it was decided that Ames and Dilling would fly to Washington at once and talk to the FBI and Central Intelligence. Their job would be to garner and piece together every scrap of information on Brungarian scientists' accomplishments.

"Let us know as soon as you get a general picture," Tom said.

Ames and Dilling promised to do so, and the meeting broke up.

Feeling somewhat reassured now that a definite plan of action had been decided upon, Tom resumed work on his sketches. Although both the problem and the solution were still hazy in his mind, a few ideas began to take shape.

A radio antenna would certainly be needed, to receive or transmit signals at a distance. And repelatron units would give the brain a way to exert force when it wanted to act. These were devices which Tom had invented to produce a repulsion-force ray. He had used the principle in both air and space flight.

A power plant might also be needed to generate additional energy in case the brain's own energy was very small. Lastly, there would have to be a control system for use either by the brain itself or by its human operators.

After an hour of work at top speed, Tom was rather pleased with one rough sketch. He was mulling over the idea when Chow Winkler and Bud Barclay wandered into the office. Both were impressed when Tom explained the sketch.

Chow stared at it, goggle-eyed at the thought of such a contraption "coming to life." "So that's the Ole Think Box, eh?" he muttered.

Tom laughed. "Good name, Chow!"

All three were startled as a voice suddenly broke in over the wall intercom. It was the operator on duty at the plant's communication center.

"Turn on your TV, skipper," the operator suggested. "We've just had a news bulletin that an earthquake tremor has been felt over in Medfield. There's a big plant there that makes rocket nose cones. A mobile TV crew's been rushed to the scene in a helicopter and they're trying to pick up the action with a television camera."

"Good night! Another quake?" Bud gasped.

Tom had already rushed to the videophone. Flicking it on, he switched to a commercial channel. Soon a picture appeared on the screen. It was a panoramic shot of a landscape, evidently viewed from a hovering aircraft, with a large industrial plant just below.

A TV commentator's voice was reporting developments. "Few visible signs of a tremor," he said. "As you can see, the rocket-plant personnel and the people of Medfield are making desperate attempts to evacuate. Fortunately, most of them have already left the immediate area."

A few cars and trucks could still be seen speeding along the ribbonlike roads within view of the hovering television camera.

"Oh - oh!" The commentator's voice broke in again. "Notice that tall stack just over the plant - see how it's starting to tremble!... It's beginning to crumble!... This must be it!"

Suddenly the whole scene seemed to explode. Plant buildings collapsed like toy houses built of cards, while at the same time huge rocks and trees were uprooted as a yawning crack opened in the ground below.

The three watchers in Tom's office stared in horrified dismay. But a moment later the picture on the TV screen became jerky and distorted, then faded out completely.

After a brief interval, a studio announcer came on. "The relay transmitter must have been knocked out by the quake. We return you now to our regularly scheduled program, but will keep you informed as bulletins come in."

"Great balls o' fire!" Chow gulped as Tom turned off

the set. "I sure hope all o' those poor folks in cars got away safe!"

Tom rushed to a wall shelf and pulled out a book on geology. He leafed quickly to a section dealing with known earthquake faults and the distribution of quakes. When he looked up at the others, his face was grim.

"What's wrong, skipper?" Bud asked tensely.

"That quake," Tom replied, "wasn't in a patterned zone any more than the Faber one was!"

Chow's jaw dropped open in a comic look of dismay. "You mean this here ole earth we live on is gettin' all busted up an' twisted around inside?"

"I wish I knew, Chow!" Tom paced worriedly about the office. "It just seems queer to me that both of those quakes should have destroyed vital defense factories!"

On a sudden impulse, Tom snatched up the telephone. His two companions listened as he put through a call to the FBI in Washington. Within moments, a friend at the Bureau, Wes Norris, came on the line.

"Look, Wes," Tom said, "is there any chance this quake that just happened at Medfield and the earlier one at Faber Electronics might have been caused by underground H-bomb blasts?"

"As a matter of fact, we're checking on that very possibility," Norris replied. "In other words, sabotage. Things are pretty hot around here since that news on Medfield came in, so I can't talk much right now, Tom.

But I can tell you this," Wes concluded, "we *are* investigating, and I do mean thoroughly!"

Bud and Chow were shocked when Tom reported his conversation with the FBI agent.

"Brand my rattlesnake stew!" Chow exploded. "Any ornery varmint that'd cause an earthquake ought to be strung up like a hoss thief!"

"I agree, Chow," Tom said. "But how do we find out for sure?"

After closing time at the plant, Bud drove home with Tom. Both Mrs. Swift and Sandy were upset as the boys discussed the situation.

"Tom, if this was deliberate," Mrs. Swift pointed out, "Enterprises may be next on the enemy's list!"

Tom did his best to allay his mother's fears, but inwardly he himself felt apprehensive. Any large-scale sabotage plot would be almost certain to include Swift Enterprises, America's most daring and advanced research center.

When his mother went upstairs to her room, Tom suggested to Bud that they drive to the nearby State Police post. Here he confided his fears to Captain Rock, an old friend of the Swifts.

"You have some request in mind?" Captain Rock inquired.

"How about making a search for any signs of suspicious digging or underground activity in the vicinity of Shopton?" Tom said. "There would have to be an excavation of some sort in order to set off an underground blast."

Captain Rock mulled over Tom's suggestion. "Sounds like a big job, but I'm afraid you're right, Tom. We can't risk a similar disaster here."

"We'd better move fast, too," Bud put in. "Those two quakes so far came only a day apart!"

Rock picked up the telephone and barked out orders. Within half an hour, several carloads of troopers were covering the outlying roads that converged on Shopton. Firemen and Chief Slater's town police force were also pressed into action. They would search every cellar in town for signs of recent digging.

Bud rode in one police car and Tom in another as a house-to-house search was conducted along the highway that ran past Enterprises.

At one weather-beaten house, where Bud stopped with a state trooper, an old man came to the door.

"What you fellers prowlin' around for?" he asked.

"Bomb emergency," the trooper said laconically. "We have orders to search every house cellar for underground openings."

Grumbling, the old man let them enter. He followed them down a rickety stairway. A moment later Bud stumbled and gave a yell. The trooper swung around just in time to see Bud drop from view!

CHAPTER V

SECRET CACHE

As the trooper's flashlight stabbed through the cellar gloom at the spot where Bud had disappeared, there came a loud splash! The light showed a round hole in the floor, rimmed by a low circle of brickwork.

"What's that hole?" the trooper snapped at the owner.

"What does it look like?" the elderly man snapped back. "It's an old well."

"A *well!*" the trooper exclaimed as he rushed to the spot. "And not even covered? What're you trying to do - kill people?"

The old man sniffed. "Used to be covered, but the lid's gone. Didn't expect to have a bunch of nosy fellers pokin' around down here!"

The state trooper muttered angrily under his breath as he shone his flashlight into the well-shaft. Bud was splashing around below, soaked and chagrined by his accident.

"Give me a hand!" he called up.

The trooper reached down, but was barely able to touch Bud's finger tips. To make matters worse, the sides of the well were slippery with moss.

"Get a rope," the trooper ordered the old man.

"Ain't got one."

The policeman reddened and stood up to his full six-foot-two. "Look, mister - what's your name?"

The elderly man shrank back, as if suspecting that the trooper's patience might have been tried too far. "Ben Smith," he mumbled.

"Okay, Mr. Smith, you get a rope or something else to pull this boy out. And fast!"

Ben Smith gulped on his chewing tobacco and hurried off. A minute or so later he returned with a length of clothesline. The trooper lowered it into the well and Bud was soon climbing out, looking like a drenched rat.

"Sorry, son," Smith said apologetically. "Guess I should have warned ye."

Bud chuckled good-naturedly. "It's all right," he said. "It was my own fault for not watching where I was going. Besides, you can't blame an American for not liking the idea of having his home searched."

The old man chuckled too and flashed a wary eye at the trooper. "I'll go get ye a towel to dry off with," he told Bud.

Meanwhile, Tom was investigating a house down the road with another state trooper. The owner, a paunchy unshaven bachelor named Pete Latty, and his seventeen-year-old nephew accompanied them to the basement.

A naked light bulb, hanging from the ceiling, revealed an ancient furnace, and an accumulation of junk. Most of it was covered with dust, but Tom noticed a large packing crate that looked as if it had been freshly moved. He walked over and began to shove the heavy box aside.

"What're you doing?" Latty asked gruffly.

"I want to look underneath," Tom replied. A second later his eyes widened as he saw a trap door, evidently leading to a subcellar.

Tom beckoned his partner over and showed his discovery. "Where does this lead to?" the trooper asked, turning back to Latty.

"Just a little storage place," the owner replied with a shrug. "I didn't think it was worth mentioning. You'd better not go down there," he added hastily. "The steps ain't safe."

"Just the same, we'll take a look," the trooper said.

"Then do it at your own risk!" Latty snapped.

The officer pulled up the trap door and Tom shone a light down. The shallow dirt-walled room below was about six feet square. On the floor, at the foot of a short rickety ladder, lay a large bundle wrapped in a tarpaulin.

Tom descended the ladder cautiously and opened the tarpaulin to see what was inside. The contents made him gasp - a large, well-oiled collection of rifles and pistols!

Looking up, Tom saw both the state trooper and Latty peering down at him - the trooper openmouthed with surprise, Latty scowling nervously.

"Don't touch 'em!" Latty warned. "Some are loaded. I keep 'em hidden for safety, but sometimes my nephew Fred here and I have target practice."

Just then Tom's keen eyes spotted a slip of paper tucked among the guns. He pulled it out. His heart gave a leap of excitement as he saw two words written on the paper - *Samson Narko!*

Hiding his amazement, Tom read the name aloud and added casually, "What's this? The make of one of the guns?"

"Uh, yeah - that's right," the man replied.

Without comment, Tom climbed out of the subcellar. As he bent down to drop the trap door, Tom flashed the officer a signal. Instantly the trooper grabbed Latty.

"Hey! Why the rough stuff?" the prisoner exclaimed. Then, as he realized the officer was about to handcuff him, the man's face turned pasty white. He pulled free from the trooper's grasp and bolted toward the stairway. His nephew stood as if paralyzed at the sudden turn of events.

Latty's attempt at flight was hopeless. Tom quickly brought him down with a flying tackle.

Later, after Latty had been manacled, Tom helped him up. "In case you don't know it," the young inventory said coldly, "your friend Narko is in jail, so you may as well talk. What's the pitch?"

Latty was trembling and still pale. "I - I d-didn't know there'd be any trouble with the cops or I'd never have done it," he quavered. "Narko offered me some dough to hide the guns. I needed money, so I took him up. That's all there was to it."

"How long have you known this Narko?" Tom asked.

"I met him a few days ago in a restaurant. Believe me, I'd never laid eyes on him before. And I wish I never had!" Latty added bitterly.

The man's story had a ring of truth. "All right, Officer, let's take him in," Tom said. To the still-astounded Fred, he added, "We're sorry about this."

Two hours later Tom and Bud sat in Chief Slater's office at Shopton police headquarters. Captain Rock and the Shopton fire chief were also on hand.

"We've had troopers, detectives, and fire inspectors swarming all over Latty's place," Captain Rock reported. "They examined his house, the garage, two sheds out back, and every inch of the grounds. But there's no indication of any place where a bomb might have been planted to cause an underground explosion in Shopton."

The fire chief nodded confirmation. "So that clue peters out," he said.

With the waning of daylight, the other groups had finally abandoned their search of the Shopton area without turning up any information. "I'll notify the FBI immediately," Chief Slater said.

Nevertheless, he promised that his men would continue their efforts the next day.

"Even if we find nothing more, that arms cache was worth all the trouble," Slater added. "The country owes you a vote of thanks, Tom. A bunch of enemy agents could have hurt a lot of people with an arsenal like that!"

"That's for sure," Captain Rock agreed. "It was a good day's haul, Tom."

The two boys drove back to the Swift home and had a quick shower. Bud borrowed clean clothes from Tom. Then they sat down to enjoy a warmed-up but tasty supper, served by Sandy and Mrs. Swift.

As they ate, the boys listened to music on the radio, interspersed with eager questions from Sandy about the bomb search.

Suddenly the radio announcer broke in. "We interrupt this broadcast to bring you an important news bulletin!"

CHAPTER VI

BRUNGARIAN COUP

Tom, Sandy, and Bud listened as the radio announcer continued:

"Reports just in say that Brungaria has been taken over by a rebel group. Military aid to support the rebel coup is pouring in from Maurevia, Brungaria's powerful province in the north. The Brungarian prime minister, his cabinet, and all loyal administrative personnel have fled or been arrested.

"Worried United States State Department officials admit that the surprise coup poses a new and dangerous threat to free-world security. Further news reports will be broadcast as soon as they reach this station," the announcer ended.

For a moment Tom and Bud were too stunned to speak. Sandy was wide-eyed with the realization that the news spelled trouble for Swift Enterprises and all America.

"Looks as though that CIA man who briefed us wasn't kidding, eh, skipper?" Bud muttered at last.

"It came sooner than he expected!" Tom said.

Jumping up from the table, Tom switched off the radio and hurried to the hall telephone. In a few moments he managed to get a long-distance call through to Wes Norris of the FBI.

"Is the news on this Brungarian coup as bad as it sounds, Wes?" Tom inquired.

"Worse! That rebel bunch really has it in for us, as you know, Tom," Norris replied. "They envy America and they'll move heaven and earth to steal our scientific secrets. This could touch off a whole epidemic of sabotage and other spy activity!"

Tom's jaw clenched grimly. He then asked the FBI man his opinion about the discovery of the secret arms cache in Pete Latty's basement.

Norris admitted he was puzzled. "It doesn't add up, Tom," the FBI agent said thoughtfully. "If our enemies were planning to destroy Shopton by a quake, why would anyone be needing a gun?"

"I can't figure it myself, Wes - unless they were planning to raid and loot Enterprises after the place was thrown into disorder," Tom deduced. "What about Narko himself? Has he talked yet?"

Norris replied that although he had not interviewed Narko himself, FBI agents who had grilled the spy had failed to elicit any information.

"Here's something else, though, which might interest you," Norris went on. "We now have reports that at the time of the Harkness and Medfield disasters, seismographs recorded simultaneous quakes off the coast of Alaska near the Aleutian chain. Tremors were also felt off the southwest coast of South America."

A new factor to consider! Tom frowned in puzzlement as he hung up the telephone after completing his talk with the FBI man.

After Tom had repeated the conversation to his companions, Bud said, "You mean the H-bomb idea goes out the window?"

Tom shrugged. "Wes says they've found no evidence to support the theory of man-produced underground blasts. It just doesn't jibe with those other remote tremors. They'd be too much of a coincidence, happening at the same time!"

"Then the quakes at Harkness and Medfield were real earthquakes!" Sandy put in.

"Looks that way," Tom admitted. "Those other tremors Wes mentioned follow a natural circum-Pacific belt which is well known to seismologists. I'm no expert, but perhaps they could have set off chain reactions below the earth's crust which triggered the two quakes in this part of the country."

In that case, the young inventor reflected, it was only a freak of nature that the Faber and nose-cone factories had been wrecked by the shock. But in spite of the seismographic clues, Tom was not entirely convinced. A nagging doubt still buzzed in the back of his mind.

The next morning Tom hurried off to his private glass-walled laboratory at Enterprises, eager to continue work on his container, or robot body, for the brain .

from space.

Tom frowned as he studied the rough sketch he had drawn in his office the afternoon before. "This setup's full of bugs!" he muttered.

Nevertheless, Tom decided, the basic idea was sound. Grabbing pencil and slide rule, he began to dash off page after page of diagrams and equations.

"Chow down!" boomed a foghorn voice. Chow Winkler, wearing a white chef's hat, wheeled a lunch cart into the lab.

"Oh... thanks." Tom scarcely looked up from his work as the cook set out an appetizing meal of Texas hash, milk, and deep-dish apple pie on the bench beside the young inventor's papers. Grumbling under his breath, Chow sauntered out.

Tom went on working intently between mouthfuls. In another hour he finished a set of pilot drawings. Then he called Hank Sterling and Arvid Hanson and asked them to come to the laboratory.

They listened with keen interest as Tom explained his latest creation.

"No telling if it will work when the energy arrives from space," Tom said, "but I think everything tracks okay. Hank, get these plans blueprinted and assign an electronics group to the project. You'd better handle the hardware yourself."

"Right." Hank rolled up the sketches.

"And, Arv," Tom went on, "I'd like a scale model made to guide them on assembly. How soon can you have it?"

Hanson promised the model for some time the next day, and the two men hurried off.

As usual, Arv proved slightly better than his word. The expert modelmaker was devoted to his craft and as apt to forget the clock as Tom himself, when absorbed in a new project. By working on in his shop long after closing hours, Hanson had a desk-size model of the space-brain robot ready for Tom's inspection when the young inventor arrived at the plant early the following morning.

"Wonderful, Arv!" Tom approved. "Every time I see one of your models of a new invention, I'm *sure* it'll work!" Hanson grinned, pleased at the compliment.

Tom hopped into a jeep and sped across the plant grounds to deliver the model to Hank Sterling and his project crew. Work was already well along on the electronic subassemblies and the strange-looking "body" was taking shape.

That afternoon Ames and Dilling returned from Washington. The report they gave to Tom bore out his hunch that the rebel Brungarian scientists might well be able to divert the space energy.

The next day was Friday. Tom was hoping, although none too optimistically, that the container might be completed before the week end. To his delight, an Enterprises pickup truck pulled up outside the laboratory later that afternoon and Hank rolled the queer-looking device inside.

"Hi, buster!" Tom greeted it. "Is this your daddy?"

Hank chuckled. "Don't look at me. It claims *you're* its daddy. But hanged if I can see much resemblance!"

"Think it'll live?"

"If not," Hank replied, only half jokingly, "the boys who worked on it will sure be disappointed. No kidding, skipper, that's quite a gadget you dreamed up!"

The device stood about shoulder-high, with a star-shaped head, one point of which could be opened. The head would contain the actual brain energy. Its upper body, cylindrical in shape and of gleaming chrome, housed the output units through which the brain would react, and also the controls. Antennas projecting out on either side gave the look of arms.

Its "waist" was girdled with a ring of repelatron radiators for exerting a repulsion force when it wanted to move, by repelling itself away from nearby objects.

Below the repelatrons was an hourglass-shaped power unit, housing a solar-charged battery.

The power unit, in turn, was mounted on a pancake-shaped transportation unit. This unit was equipped with both casters and a sort of caterpillar-crawler arrangement for the contrivance to get about over obstacles. Inside was a gyro-stabilizer to keep the whole device upright.

Tom felt a glow of pride - and eager impatience - as he inspected the device. If it worked as he hoped, this odd creature might one day provide earth scientists with a priceless store of information about intelligent life on Planet X!

Bud and Chow, entering the laboratory soon after Hank Sterling had left, found Tom still engrossed in his thoughts.

"Wow! Is this your spaceman?" Bud inquired.

Tom nodded, then grinned at his callers' gaping expressions. Each was trying to imagine how the "thing" would look in action.

"Sure is a queer-lookin' buckaroo!" Chow commented, when Tom finished explaining how it was supposed to work.

On a sudden impulse, the old cowpoke took off his ten-gallon hat and plumped it on the creature. Then he removed his polka-dotted red bandanna and knotted it like a neckerchief just below the star head.

Tom laughed heartily as Bud howled, "Ride 'em, spaceman!"

Tom was eager to notify his mysterious space friends that the container was now ready to receive the brain energy. Bud went with him by jeep to the space-communications laboratory. Chow, however, stayed behind and stared in fascination at the odd-looking robot creature.

The stout cook walked back and forth, eying the thing

suspiciously from every angle. "Wonder what the critter eats?" he muttered.

Feeling in his shirt pocket, Chow brought out a wad of his favorite bubble gum. Should he or shouldn't he? "Shucks, won't hurt to try," the old Texan decided.

Chow unlocked the hinged point of the star head and popped the gum inside. He was somewhat disappointed when nothing happened. Feeling a trifle foolish, Chow finally removed his hat and bandanna from the creature and stumped off.

Meanwhile, in the space-communications laboratory, Tom was pounding out a message on the keyboard of the electronic brain. Tom had invented this device for automatically coding and decoding messages between the Swifts and their space friends. It was connected to a powerful transmitting-and-receiving apparatus, served by a huge radio-telescope antenna mounted atop the communications building.

Bud looked on as Tom signaled:

TOM SWIFT TO SPACE FRIENDS. CONTAINER FOR ENERGY IS NOW READY. SHOULD IT BE PLACED OUTDOORS?

Stirred by a worrisome afterthought, Tom added:

MESSAGES MAY BE INTERCEPTED BY ENEMY WHO WISHES TO STEAL ENERGY. SUGGEST YOU USE FLIGHT PATH TO LAND EXACTLY TWO MILES WEST OF FIRST CONTACT WITH US.

"By 'first contact,' you mean when that black missile landed at Enterprises?" Bud asked.

Tom nodded. At that time, he reminded Bud, the Brungarians and their conquerors had not yet learned of the Swifts' communication from another planet. Hence they would have no idea of the site referred to – which would hamper any plans to kidnap the brain energy.

"I get it," Bud said. "Smart idea, pal!"

Tensely the two boys waited for a reply from outer space.

CHAPTER VII

WALL OF WATER!

Minutes went by before the signal bell rang on the electronic brain. Both Tom and Bud dashed over to the machine as it began to spell out the incoming message on tape:

> ENERGY WILL COME TO THE SPOT YOU SUGGESTED. WE CAN CONTROL FLIGHT COURSE BUT WHILE THE ENERGY IS ON EARTH YOU WILL BE IN CHARGE. WE WILL HAVE NO CONTROL FOR TWENTY-ONE DAYS. THEN WE WILL RECALL ENERGY TO BRING US IMPRESSIONS AND DATA OF YOUR WORLD.

The two boys stared at each other excitedly as the transmission ended.

"Wow!" Bud murmured. "If Planet X is a peaceful place, Ole Think Box is sure in for a jolt here on earth!"

Tom grinned fleetingly at the reference to Chow's nickname for the robot creature. Then he became serious, knowing that Bud's words were all too true. The space visitor might also take back impressions of the suffering and warlike threats that some earth countries inflict on one another. Maybe one day, Tom reflected, it would be different.

In the meantime, the young inventor realized he had an awesome responsibility. He must not only make the best use of the brain energy during its stay on earth, but also keep it from falling into the hands of treacherous Brungarian plotters.

Tom's thoughts were suddenly interrupted by the sound of girls' voices. Sandy and Phyl were standing in the doorway of the space-communications laboratory.

"Talk about deep thinkers!" Sandy said teasingly.

"Goodness, we had no idea we'd be interrupting a session of the brain trust," Phyl added with a mischievous sparkle in her brown eyes. "Maybe we should go away again, Sandy!"

"Hey! Hold it, you two!" Bud exclaimed. "What do you think, Tom - are these the visitors we've been expecting from outer space?"

"Well! I like that!" Sandy pouted. "Do we look like a couple of little green people?"

Tom chuckled and seized the opportunity to do a little teasing of his own. "I think it's just your pointed heads that fooled us, Sis." Then, as the two girls broke down in laughter, he added, "Why the unexpected visit?"

Sandy and Phyl explained that they had come to invite the boys to a picnic cruise on Lake Carlopa the next day.

"And while we're here, since it's practically quitting time anyhow," Sandy went on, her blue eyes twinkling, "we might even let you drive us some place for dinner."

"Guess they've trapped us, Bud," Tom said with a grin. "Okay, it's a deal. But first we have something to show you." He took the girls to his laboratory to show them the robot creature.

"It's marvelous!" Sandy exclaimed, and Phyl agreed.

Early the next morning Bud called for Tom and Sandy in his tomato-red convertible. Then they stopped at the Newtons' house to pick up Phyl. Each girl had packed a picnic basket for the day's sail.

"Hmm. Looks as though we're going to be well fed," Bud commented jokingly. "What's on the menu, girls?"

"Chicken and ham sandwiches..." Sandy began.

"Pickles, olives, hard-boiled eggs, potato salad..." Phyl went on.

"Chocolate cake, milk..." Sandy took up the list.

"Stop! You have us hungry as bears already!" Tom warned.

"Right!" Bud agreed. "Come on! Let's get this cruise under way!"

The two couples drove to the Shopton Yacht Club dock on Lake Carlopa. There they boarded the *Sunspot*, a beautiful thirty-foot sailing ketch with auxiliary engine which Mr. Swift and Mr. Newton had purchased for a frequently promised but not yet realized joint family vacation.

The craft was equipped with twin gravitex stabilizers, mounted one on each side of the hull. These gave it amazing smoothness even when plowing through rough seas. They were adaptations of a device Tom had invented for his space kite and *Cosmic Sailer*.

"Oh, what a gorgeous day for a sail!" Phyl said, aglow with enthusiasm.

The sky was a cloudless blue. Under a hot summer sun, a brisk breeze was ruffling the lake into tiny whitecaps. The two couples cast off eagerly and were soon scudding out across the water under full sail.

Tom and Bud wore swimming trunks under their slacks. Unfortunately the girls had forgotten to bring their suits. When the *Sunspot* reached the center of the lake, the boys hove to, stripped down to their trunks, and dived overboard. Meanwhile, the girls sun-bathed on deck. Soon it was time for the picnic lunch, and all four ate with healthy young appetites.

"Jeepers!" Sandy whispered to Phyl with a giggle. "After a feast like this, we'll have to go on a diet!"

"Don't say it," Phyl warned, "or Tom and Bud will use that as an excuse for never taking us out ag -"

She broke off with a gasp.

"What's wrong?" Tom asked.

Breathless with fright, Phyl pointed off to starboard. The others paled. An enormous wave was sweeping across the lake, straight toward the ketch!

"Jumpin' jets!" Bud gulped. "It's like a tidal wave!"

The boat was already rocking under the swells that preceded the oncoming huge breaker.

"Quick!" Tom yelled. "Grab life jackets while I start the engine!"

The four leaped into action. Every instant the terrifying wave rushed closer! By now it was a twelve-foot wall of water!

Tom and the others had just put on the jackets and the engine had barely gunned into life when disaster struck. The mammoth wave swept up the *Sunspot* and heeled it far over into the trough like a toy bark. The next instant a cataract of water poured over the deck with stunning force!

"We're going under!" Phyl screamed.

All four were swept overboard in the maelstrom! Under the smashing impact of the water, the ketch's mainmast bent and groaned. A moment later came a crack like a gunshot. The mast broke off, hung teetering by shreds, then toppled into the water. As it fell, the mast struck Sandy a grazing blow on the head!

"Sandy!" Bud cried fearfully as he struggled in the swirling torrent.

Calling on every ounce of strength, he swam with

powerful strokes toward the girl. Sandy was dazed and limp. Bud's husky arm circled her tightly. Then he began to fight his way toward shore. Tom and Phyl - each struggling in the turbulent water - could only breathe a prayer of thanks as they watched the rescue.

As the huge wave raced shoreward, the lake water gradually became calmer in its wake. Tom was able to assist Phyl, and Sandy by now had recovered her faculties.

The *Sunspot* had capsized but could still be seen afloat, some distance away. Rather than swim to it and cling to the hulk in the hope that a rescue boat would arrive, the four decided to continue on toward shore. They knew that the aftermath of the tidal wave would keep all shore facilities in an uproar for hours to come.

As they neared the beach, the young people could see other overturned craft and heads bobbing in the water. A few daring persons finally began putting out in motorboats and rowboats to pick up the survivors.

A hundred yards from shore, one of the boats took Tom's group aboard. Minutes later, they were scrambling out onto a dock.

"Are you all right, Sandy?" Bud asked, his arm still around her.

"I - I think so," she gasped weakly, "but I must have swallowed half the lake!"

"Take it easy, Sis!" Tom added, as Sandy swayed and shuddered from the shock of her recent ordeal.

Gently he made Sandy lie down and pillowed her head on a folded tarpaulin provided by the sympathetic boatman. Phyl, though wan and white-faced, was in somewhat better shape.

"Tom, we must get these girls home as soon as possible," Bud declared.

This, however, was not easily accomplished. The tidal wave had caused devastation along the entire shore front. Many docks had been wrecked, boats splintered like matchsticks, and buildings along the water smashed.

When Tom's group reached Bud's convertible, parked near the yacht club pier, they found the car completely waterlogged. Its electrical system gave not even a faint sputter or spark.

"Oh, fine!" Bud groaned. "The crowning touch!"

Eventually ambulances and private cars began to arrive to transport the injured. Tom, Bud, and the two girls were given a lift to the Swift home where Sandy and Phyl were immediately put to bed by a worried Mrs. Swift.

Downstairs, Tom switched on the TV set. A mobile camera crew from the local station was scanning the water front and interviewing witnesses of the disaster. To the two boys, the most interesting note came in a statement by the announcer that a very slight earth tremor had been felt in Shopton.

"But no damage occurred except along the water front," the announcer explained.

Tom gave a snort of anger, jumped up from his chair, and began pacing about the living room. "Bud, I feel sure that wall of water was caused by a minor earthquake!" the young inventor declared. "What's more, I'll bet it was *man-made!*"

Bud stared at his friend, appalled but feeling a hot surge of anger himself. "If you're right, pal, it's the most fiendish sabotage I've ever heard of! Think of all the lives that were endangered!"

Tom nodded grimly. "I *am* thinking!"

Both boys jerked around to look at the TV set again as a studio announcer's voice suddenly broke into the telecast:

"Flash! A severe quake has occurred at the head-quarters of the American Archives Foundation, a hundred miles from Shopton. The Foundation's buildings, containing many priceless government and scientific documents, were badly damaged, and an underground microfilm vault was utterly destroyed. Apparently this quake was part of the tremor felt here at Shopton."

Within minutes the Swifts' home phone began jangling constantly. Some calls were from friends, others from strangers. Many of the calls were routed through from the Enterprises switchboard.

One was from Dan Perkins of the *Shopton Bulletin.* "What about it, Tom?" the editor demanded. "I guess you know by now the public's aroused and in a state of near panic over all these quakes. What they all want to know is this: are you, Tom Swift, going to find a way to stop all this destruction?"

Tom's jaw jutted out angrily. "Yes, I am!" he snapped. "And you can quote me on that!"

CHAPTER VIII

A SUSPECT TALKS

The next morning Tom was up at the crack of dawn, grimly determined to find an answer to the earthquake menace. He ate a hasty breakfast, then drove to his private laboratory at Enterprises. He instructed the switchboard operator to shut off all incoming calls, then plunged into a study of the mystifying problem.

Earthquake activity, Tom knew, tends to occur in circular patterns, like bands around the earth - for instance, the circum-Pacific belt, and another belt extending eastward from the Mediterranean through Asia and on into the East Indies. Often these quake lines are visible as breaks or ruptures along the ground surface, called *fault traces*. No doubt, Tom thought, there were many more uncharted ones.

Could an enemy scientist be making use of these earth faults to produce a man-made quake? Tom mulled over the disturbing idea.

"How would I tackle the job myself, if I had to undertake such a project for national defense?" the young inventor mused. He felt a growing sense of excitement as an idea began to take shape in his mind.

What about an artificial shock wave!

An hour later Bud Barclay walked into the laboratory and found Tom hunched over a jumbled pile of reference books on his workbench.

"What cooks, skipper?" Bud asked.

Tom looked up, his blue eyes blazing. "Bud, I think I may have the answer!"

Tom got up from his stool and paced about the laboratory. "Suppose the Brungarian rebel scientists have invented some sort of shock-wave producer - a device for sending vibrations through the earth's crust or the mantle underneath."

"Okay, suppose they have," Bud replied.

Tom snatched up a piece of chalk and made some quick diagrams on a blackboard. "Just this, pal. Let's say they set up two or three stations around the world for sending out such waves in a definite direction. Wherever the wave crosses an earth fault or another wave - *boom!* An earthquake!"

Bud stared. "No kidding, is that how those rats triggered off all these quakes?"

"It must be," Tom declared. "It's the only possible explanation."

"Good night!" Bud gasped weakly. "What a weapon! Just push a button every so often and you could blow up another country bit by bit - and no one could ever prove who was behind the attack!"

Victor Appleton

Tom nodded. "Enough to make every American shiver, if he only knew!"

"What can we do about it?" Bud asked.

Tom resumed his worried pacing. "I'll have to invent a shock-wave deflector, Bud. It must be done in a hurry, too. Our enemy may start to destroy American cities as well as vital defense plants!"

Immediately Tom put through an urgent call to an eminent scientist in Washington who was a member of the National Research Council. Quickly he outlined a plan.

"Tom, I'll talk to the president's special science adviser at once," the man promised. "I'll try to set up a meeting for ten o'clock tomorrow morning at Enterprises."

Feeling relieved, Tom left the plant with Bud. The two boys drove off to attend church with Mrs. Swift and Sandy. Then, after the Sunday midday meal, Tom returned to his laboratory to work on ideas for a shock-wave deflector.

Bud and Sandy, meanwhile, drove to the Shopton Yacht Club to inspect the damage to the *Sunspot*. Tom had arranged with a salvage crew to tow the disabled ketch back to its slip.

Monday morning, a sleek Air Force jet transport touched down at Swift Enterprises. Aboard were a select group of top government scientists. Tom and Bud greeted them as they disembarked on the runway, then drove them to a conference room in the Enterprises main building.

"I'd say your theory is right, Tom, about the quakes being produced by artificial shock waves," said Bernt Ahlgren, a tall, hawk-faced man with a shock of red hair. He was a member of the Defense Department's Advanced Research Projects Agency. "But how do we stop them?"

"I believe they can be damped out by opposing waves," Tom replied. "This is assuming that I can design the right sort of equipment to do the job - and also that we can set up a warning system to alert us of the enemy shock waves in time." The young inventor sketched out the sort of shock-wave deflector which he had in mind. The government experts were very much impressed. In the session that followed, the visiting scientists contributed many tips and suggestions. Tom noted them down gratefully.

After a thorough discussion, it was agreed that the Defense Department would set up detectors at fifty check points around the country. Tom would choose the exact spots. Detection data from the check points would be fed to an electronic computer. The computer would establish the pattern, if any, of incoming enemy shock waves.

Dr. Gregg Miles, a seismologist from the Bureau of Mines, agreed to take on the job of setting up the check points.

"Thanks for your prompt co-operation," Tom said, smiling gratefully as the meeting broke up.

"We should thank you, Tom, for coming up with a plan to cope with this fiendish threat," Ahlgren replied. The others heartily agreed.

Shortly after lunch, Tom was hard at work in his laboratory when the telephone rang. It was Chief Slater at Shopton police headquarters.

"You'd better get over here fast, Tom," Slater said. "Samson Narko is ready to talk!"

Tom needed no urging. "Right, Chief!"

As he drove into Shopton, Tom wondered what the Brungarian agent would reveal. Was it possible that he might tip off the whole secret behind the destructive man-made earthquakes?

Chief Slater was waiting in his office. "Narko showed signs of cracking this morning," Slater told Tom, "so I notified the Central Intelligence Agency. They're flying a man up here - in fact he should be here by now. Narko won't talk till he arrives."

"How come?" Tom asked.

"Narko wants a bargain," Slater explained. "If the government will promise to deport him at once without trial, he'll spill what he knows."

Tom whistled. "I sure wouldn't want to be in *his* shoes when he gets back to Brungaria! His bosses aren't stupid. They'll know he must have made a deal to get off scot free!"

Just then a taxi from the airport pulled up outside police headquarters, and the CIA official was ushered into Slater's office. He proved to be John Thurston.

"Narko's waiting in his cell," Slater said, after an

exchange of handshakes. "Let's hope he hasn't changed his mind."

The Brungarian spy rose from his cot as the turnkey unlocked his cell door.

"You are from Washington, eh?" Narko said to Thurston. "Very well. I presume the police have told you my offer. Is it a bargain?"

Thurston was poker-faced. "You know the penalty for spying!" he snapped. "In your own country it would mean death. Why should we let you off?"

Narko's calmness evaporated. Beads of sweat burst out on his forehead.

"I have done no harm and I know little or nothing of my superiors' plans!" the spy said excitedly. "Why should I lie to you with my life at stake? After all, I am only an insignificant agent. But one important thing I do know - and this I will reveal if you promise to deport me at once!"

Thurston eyed him coldly. "Very well," the CIA man decided. "You have my word."

Narko sat down on his cot, breathing heavily. Then he looked up at the three Americans. "Your nation's capital, Washington, D.C., is going to be blown up!" the Brungarian asserted.

His words struck like a bombshell. Chief Slater and John Thurston stared at Narko in open-mouthed astonishment.

Then Slater scowled. "What a preposterous story! I suppose they're going to fly a plane over and drop an atom bomb - just like that!" He snapped his fingers.

Thurston was also inclined to doubt Narko's story. Any such bold move by the Brungarians, he declared, would amount to an act of war.

"It is the truth!" Narko shouted. "Do not forget - you have made a promise."

Tom Swift did not share Chief Slater's and Thurston's skepticism. Narko's words had chilled him with dismay. He called the other two aside and gave them a quick whispered briefing on the theory he had discussed with the government scientists, asking them to keep it confidential.

If the Brungarians indeed had a means of producing artificial shock waves, Tom pointed out, they could easily destroy Washington without the slightest risk to themselves.

Both Thurston and Chief Slater were alarmed. Turning back to Narko, they grilled him for clues. But it seemed obvious that the Brungarian was telling all he knew - or, at any rate, all he intended to reveal.

"We're wasting our time," Thurston said finally, with a look of disgust. "But I made a promise in the name of the United States government and the promise will be kept."

Turning to Chief Slater, the CIA man added, "Turn him over to the FBI and have them take him to New York. I'll arrange for a seat on the first plane for Brungaria."

Tom drove back thoughtfully to Enterprises. Bud was waiting in his laboratory with news.

"Your dad went from Washington to Fearing Island and has gone up to your space outpost," Bud reported. "He has to do some experiments for the government project he's working on."

The outpost was a space station which Tom Swift Jr. had built 22,300 miles above the earth. It was a production factory for his famous solar batteries, and also an immensely valuable setup for space research and exploration.

"Think I'll radio Dad and let him know what's going on," Tom decided. "He may have some good suggestions. He usually does!"

Tom warmed up his private transmitter-receiver and beamed out a code call through the automatic scrambler. Seconds later, the loud-speaker crackled in response.

But just as the outpost operator's voice came through, the radio set exploded in Tom's face!

CHAPTER IX

THE CAVE MONSTER

"Skipper!" Bud cried anxiously as Tom staggered back, his hands to his face.

"I'm all right - no harm done," Tom assured his friend.

Both boys were a bit shaken by the accident, nevertheless. Chow came rushing in as Bud was brushing the fragments of debris from Tom's clothes and examining the young inventor's face.

"Brand my flyin' flapjacks, what happened?" Chow asked. The chef had been bringing a tray of fruit juice to the laboratory and had heard the explosion outside.

"The radio set just blew up in my face," Tom explained. "Fortunately, the equipment was transistorized mostly with printed circuits. Otherwise," he added, "I might have been badly cut by slivers of glass from the exploding vacuum tubes."

As it was, the young inventor had suffered only a few slight scratches and a bruise on the temple from a piece of the shattered housing. Bud swabbed Tom's injuries with antiseptic from the first-aid cabinet while Chow poured out glasses of grape juice.

"What caused it, Tom?" Bud asked as they paused to sip the fruit drink.

"Good question," Tom replied. "Frankly, I don't know." But he was wondering if the set might have been sabotaged.

Tom was still eager to get in touch with his father and telephoned the electronics department to bring another set to his laboratory. Chow left just as the new set arrived.

Tom hooked it up quickly, donned a set of goggles, and tuned to the space-station frequency. Then he picked up the microphone and stepped well back from the set, waving Bud out of range at the same time.

"Tom Swift calling Outpost!... Come in, please!"

A moment later came another explosion! *The new set had also blown up!*

"Good night!" Bud gasped in a stunned voice. "Don't tell me that's just a coincidence!"

Tom shrugged. "We can certainly rule out the possibility that anything was wrong with the radio itself. Every set is checked before it leaves the electronics department."

"So where does that leave us?" Bud persisted.

Tom shook his head worriedly as he took off the goggles. "Both times it seemed to happen just as the reply was coming through from the space station. There is no possibility that their signal was too strong -

in other words, that the explosion was caused by overloading the receiving circuits."

"Are you implying that an enemy intercepted the message and sent some sort of ray that caused the set to explode?" Bud demanded.

Tom's face showed clearly that Bud had pinpointed the suspicion in the young inventor's mind. "Could be."

Bud was worried by this latest development. "Skipper, suppose I hop up to the space wheel and talk it over with your dad. He may be able to help us detect any enemy moves."

"Good idea, pal," Tom agreed. "The sooner the better, I'd say."

The boys exchanged a quick handshake and affectionate shoulder slaps. Then Bud hurried out to one of the Enterprises hangars to ready a helijet for the flight to Fearing Island. This was the Swifts' rocket base, just off the Atlantic coast. From there, Bud would board one of the regular cargo shuttle rockets operating between the space station and Fearing.

Tom, meanwhile, plunged back to work on his shock-wave deflector.

At ten the next morning he called in Hank Sterling and showed him a set of completed drawings.

"Hank, you did a fast job on the container for the brain," Tom began apologetically, "but you'll really have to burn out a bearing on this one!"

Hank grinned. "I'm geared to action. Say, what do we call it, anyhow?" he asked.

Tom grinned. "Chow told me last night this gadget looked like a fireplug under a rose trellis and I ought to call it Fireplug Rose! But I've given it a more dignified name - the Quakelizor, which stands for an underground quake wave deflector."

Briefly, Tom explained the various parts of his latest invention, which consisted of a hydrant-sized cylinder to be inserted into the ground, with magnetic coils near the top. A smaller hydraulic cylinder, mounted above this, was wired to a metal framework and radio transmitter.

"This setup will detect any incoming enemy shock waves," Tom said. "We'll need fifty of 'em, so turn the job over to Swift Construction. And have Uncle Ned put on extra shifts."

The Swift Construction Company, managed by Ned Newton, was the commercial division which mass-produced Tom Jr.'s and Tom Sr.'s inventions.

Information from the detector-transmitters, Tom went on, would be fed into an electronic computer at the Bureau of Mines in Washington.

The Quakelizor itself was housed in a massive cube-shaped casting with two large spheres mounted on top. From each of its four sides jutted a hydraulic piston.

"How does it work, Tom?" Hank asked.

"Dual-control spheres on top," Tom explained, "will

receive by radio signal the pulse frequency computed in Washington."

He added that inside each sphere was a "pulsemaker." This would produce changes in the pressure of the hydraulic fluid by affecting the kinetic energy of the fluid's atoms.

The pressure changes would then be enormously magnified in the four hydraulic output drivers. When the unit was embedded in rock, underground, the huge pistons would send out counter shock waves through the earth's crust to neutralize the enemy waves.

"Wow!" Hank Sterling was breathless at the sheer scope of the young scientist's newest invention. "I'll get hot on the job right away."

After forty-eight hours of round-the-clock work, the equipment was ready. Tom conferred by telephone with both Dr. Miles in the Bureau of Mines and Bernt Ahlgren in the Pentagon. He had already chosen the spots for the detector-transmitter check points.

Tom told the men that he believed the best spot for the Quakelizor itself was on a certain government reservation in Colorado. A deep underground cave there would provide a perfect site.

"We'll be close enough to the San Andreas fault to prevent a really huge-scale disaster," Tom explained. "And the Rocky Mountain structure will give us a good bedrock medium for shooting out waves anywhere across the continent."

Dr. Miles and Ahlgren agreed enthusiastically. Tom

and the two scientists spoke over a three-way telephone hookup - with automatic scramblers to counter the danger of enemy monitors - laying plans to install the equipment. Ahlgren agreed to fly a technical crew out to the spot in Colorado which Tom had named.

The next day, Tom, Hank, and several top Enterprises' engineers, including Art Wiltessa, took off in the *Sky Queen*. This was Tom's huge atomic-powered Flying Lab. The massive plane flew at supersonic speeds and was equipped with jet lifters for vertical take-off or hovering.

A Whirling Duck heliplane, loaded with communications equipment, accompanied the *Sky Queen*. In little more than an hour, the two craft touched down in a rugged Colorado canyon. The government technical crew was already on hand.

"Glad to know you," Tom said, shaking hands with the engineer in charge. He introduced his own men and added, "Better roll up your sleeves. This job is going to take plenty of oomph!"

The parts of the Quakelizor were unloaded from the *Sky Queen* onto dollies. Then the group, armed with bull's-eye lanterns, flashlights, and walkie-talkies, hauled the parts by tractor into the cave.

"Okay. Now let's pick out the spot for embedding the unit," Tom said.

The men had no sooner begun to look around the huge underground chamber when a fearsome growl rumbled through the cave. Everyone whirled about and the next instant froze in horror.

A huge bear reared up in the mouth of the cave! The monster snarled and blinked its yellow eyes in the glare of lights.

"We're trapped!" Hank cried out.

The enormous bruin was now waving his huge head from side to side, as if daring the intruders to step up and fight.

Several of the government men had brought rifles and shotguns. But in spite of their peril, no one wanted to shoot the handsome old fellow.

"I'll send out an SOS," Tom said. "If help arrives before the bear attacks, we won't use guns."

He radioed the local Forest Ranger post. After a nerve-racking wait, with the group expecting a charge from the beast at any minute, two rangers appeared and captured the bear with a net. One man of the government work crew knocked together a stout wooden cage. The beast, outraged, was loaded aboard the heliplane to be released in an area remote from the cave.

Now the grueling job of installing the Quakelizor began. First the cave was cleared of debris, bats, and other small living creatures. Then a site was marked out on the cave floor. Tom had brought along a midget model of his great atomic earth blaster, which he had invented to drill for iron at the South Pole.

With the blaster, Tom quickly drilled a pit of exact size

into the bedrock. Then the Quakelizor was assembled and lowered into place by a portable crane. A power plant and radio antenna were set up and the installation was finally completed.

"I must return to Shopton now," Tom said. "Art here will stick around and help you operate the setup," he told the government engineers after radio contact had been made with Washington. "If anything goes wrong, just flash word to Enterprises."

The *Sky Queen* and the heliplane sped back across the continent. As Tom landed at Enterprises he was greeted by Bud, who came speeding out on the airfield by jeep.

"Just got back from the space wheel about an hour ago," Bud said. "Your dad's really worried about those exploding radio sets, Tom. He has no clues, but he's sure the scientists working for the Brungarian rebel setup are responsible. He thinks they may try to ruin all of Enterprises' communications system by remote control."

Tom's face was grave as he listened. The two boys discussed the problem as they drove to the Swifts' office in the main building.

"Boy, I sure wish I could think of some way to cope with it," Tom said wearily, flopping down in his desk chair.

"Your dad said to give it the old college try," Bud reported. "And he also said he'd be back in two days to help you on the problem."

Tom glanced at the calendar. "Which reminds me," he said, "on Monday the brain energy will be due from space!"

The thought sent a thrill of excitement tinged with worry through the young inventor's mind. Would the container he had devised prove suitable?

"Hey! A call on the videophone!" Bud pointed to the red light flashing on the control board. He jumped up and switched on the set.

Blake, the Washington announcer, appeared on the screen.

"Bad news, skipper," he said ominously. "An earthquake tremor was just felt here in Washington. It centered in a shipyard on the Potomac and caused great damage!"

CHAPTER X

ENERGY FROM PLANET X

Tom and Bud listened in dismay as Blake reported all the details he had been able to gather.

"Was my Quakelizor a flop, Bud?" Tom muttered, his shoulders drooping as the announcer signed off. "It must have been!"

"Don't be silly! Snap out of it!" Bud gave his pal a cheerful poke in the ribs, hoping to buck him up. "You heard what Blake said - Washington itself was hardly touched. Without your setup, think of all the people that *might* have been killed or injured! And all the government buildings that might have been wrecked, maybe even the White House. I'd say your shock-wave deflector must have been at least ninety per cent effective!"

Tom brightened somewhat on hearing Bud's words. He picked up the phone, and placed a call to Dr. Miles at the Bureau of Mines. It was almost half an hour before the operator was able to get a line through. But Tom felt the suspense had been worth while when Dr. Miles exclaimed:

"Tom, it was a miracle you completed the Quakelizor

installation in time! In all probability it saved us from a major national disaster, perhaps worse than Pearl Harbor!"

Tom felt a glow of pride and relief. "Thanks, sir. But what about the shipyard destruction?" he added, still not entirely convinced.

"That was a bad break, Tom," Dr. Miles admitted. "Our detectors showed that the shock waves had been almost damped out when a sudden power failure occurred. It turned out that an overload had shorted the Quakelizor's power plant. The crew had it fixed within moments, but by that time the damage was done."

Tom winced as he heard of the unfortunate accident, but was thankful the results had been no worse.

Miles went on to say that he had just been conferring with Ahlgren at the Pentagon. The Defense Department now feared that attempts might be made against other large cities and was therefore eager to have Tom deliver several quake deflectors as soon as possible. These would be installed at strategic points around the country.

"The government heads were so impressed with your invention, Tom," Dr. Miles added, "that they'll probably be walking the floor anxiously until the others arrive."

Tom chuckled, then became serious. "Tell them we'll go to work right away," he informed the seismologist. "I'll have the new Quakelizors ready as soon as possible, but you'd better warn your associates it's bound to take a few days."

As soon as the conversation was completed, Tom dialed Ned Newton at the Swift Construction Company. Although he was actually not a relative of the Swifts, both Tom and Sandy had from childhood called him "Uncle Ned."

"What's up, Tom?" he asked.

Tom told him of the latest request from Washington and asked that another three-shift work schedule be set up to turn out the additional Quakelizors.

"Hank and I will bring the blueprints over right away, if you don't mind being late to dinner," Tom said.

Ned Newton agreed willingly, only too happy to help cope with the quake menace. By eight o'clock that evening, work on the project was proceeding at great speed. The Swift Construction Company continued humming with activity around the clock.

The week end was almost over by the time Mr. Swift arrived back from the space station. Tom flew to Fearing Island to meet him. On the short hop back to Enterprises, they discussed the radio problem.

"I think the solution's been staring us in the face, Dad, but we've been too worried to think of it," Tom said. "Remember Li Ching's jamming-wave generator?"

He was referring to a device used recently by an Oriental foe of Tom and his father. Mr. Swift's eyes lighted up with a quick flash of understanding.

"Dad, you wrote a report on the generator for the government with a memo on possible ways to combat it," Tom went on. "Maybe the same measures would work in this case."

The Swifts had discovered that their enemy had been intercepting Tom's messages, thereby learning the frequency to which the Swifts' receiver was tuned. They then radiated a signal at this frequency, modulated at the frequency to which the local oscillator was set. This had caused a buildup of energy in the I.F. transformers, resulting in their explosion.

Now Mr. Swift said, "You're right, son. We'll insert a blocking filter in the R.F. stage that should do the trick."

Their minds relieved of this problem, the Swifts were eagerly looking forward to the arrival of the brain energy from space the next day. The scheduled time, if pinpointed at exactly two weeks from the moment when the first message was received, would be half an hour past noon.

The spot, two miles from Enterprises, was on a lonely hillside. It was shaded by trees, higher up the slope, with bushes and other wild-growing greenery softening its contours. Over the week end, Tom had had carpenters from Enterprises put up a small cabin at the foot.

As twelve-thirty approached, Tom, Bud, Mr. Swift, Hank Sterling, Arv Hanson, and several other Swift technicians stood by at the scene with the star-headed container. Chow had also begged to be on hand.

"I jest got to see Ole Think Box come to life!" he said.

Eyes darted back and forth from wrist watches to sky as the zero moment ticked closer. Bud even began muttering a countdown.

"X minus three... X minus two... X minus one... This is it!"

All eyes flashed skyward. *But nothing happened!* Not a speck showed in the blue, cloudless sky.

The watchers glanced at one another uncertainly. More minutes went by. Soon it was quarter to one... then one o'clock.

"No mistake about the time, was there?" Arv asked.

Mr. Swift shook his head. "Not if the code was translated correctly." He frowned. "It's true they spoke merely in terms of days. But their time references are usually very precise."

The waiting group fidgeted and prowled back and forth to ease their tension. Feelings of suspense began changing into gloom after two more hours had passed with no sign from the sky.

Disappointed but unable to wait any longer, the technical men went back to the plant, one by one. Hank Sterling, too, and Arv Hanson finally had to leave.

"Sorry, skipper," Hank muttered. "Ring us right away if it shows up."

"Sure, Hank."

Victor Appleton

As six o'clock went by, Chow tried to pep up his companions' drooping spirits with a simple but tasty supper, warmed up on an electric hot plate in the cabin.

"What do you think, skipper? Are we out of luck?" Bud asked as they ate.

"Our space friends haven't let us down yet," Tom replied. "I'm sure they won't this time." Though he didn't say so aloud, Tom was worried that their Brungarian enemies might have managed to divert and capture the energy.

Mr. Swift seemed to read Tom's thoughts. "Let's hope no hitch has occurred," he said quietly.

The sun went down. Twilight slowly deepened. The trees on the hillside faded from view in the gathering darkness.

"*There it is!*" Bud yelled suddenly.

Electrified, the four sprang up in an instant. A speck of light was sailing across the sky! But their faces fell as it drew closer.

"Only an airplane," Bud grumbled.

At ten o'clock Mr. Swift gave a weary yawn. "The spirit is willing but the flesh is weak," he confessed. "I got only two hours of sleep on the space wheel, and apparently last night wasn't enough to catch up. Sorry, fellows."

"Why don't you go home, Dad? Hit the hay," Tom said sympathetically.

Promising to take a turn on watch if the vigil continued through the next day, Mr. Swift drove off in his car.

Time dragged by slowly as the three remaining watchers chatted and looked hopefully at the stars. Eventually Chow propped himself against a tree and dropped off to sleep to the accompaniment of low-droning snores. Bud too began to drowse.

It was long past midnight when Tom suddenly caught sight of a moving light in the sky. He stiffened and held his breath. Another false alarm?

But no! A glowing, faintly bluish mass with a comet tail of luminous orange red was slowly proceeding through the pattern of stars!

"Hey, fellows! Wake up!" Tom shouted. He sprang to his feet and unlatched a single point of the star head. Within seconds, Bud and Chow were both wide awake, as excited as Tom. The blue nebulous mass moved closer and closer. The three watchers were speechless with awe.

As the ball of energy descended toward them, it lit up the whole scene. The hillside looked almost as if it were on fire. The earth vibrated, and the air had the sharp smell of ozone. This was followed by a frightening clatter and rumble. The force of the energy was sweeping down rocks, gravel, and shrubbery in a hillside avalanche!

"Look out!" Chow shrieked. "We'll be pulverized in this rock stampede!" He streaked for cover as a huge boulder came plunging straight toward him.

"Hold fast, Bud!" Tom cried. "Nothing's headed our way!"

Steeling his nerves, he grabbed the waiting container and held on grimly. An instant later the glowing mass sharpened and narrowed itself into a snakelike bolt of fire that arced straight into the head of Tom's invention.

Tom gave a yell of triumph and clamped the star point shut, then pushed a button to activate the self-sealing process.

Chow peered out cautiously from behind a clump of rock. The next second, he let out a Texas whoop, bounded from cover like an over-sized gnome, and sent his ten-gallon hat sailing high into the air.

"*Yippee!*"

Bud cheered too. "The visitor from Planet X has arrived!"

In their excitement and relief, the three hugged one another and jumped for joy.

"Should we wake up your dad and tell him the good news - or keep it a surprise till morning?" Bud asked Tom.

"I guess we'd better -"

Tom broke off in a gasp as the robotlike container suddenly began to whirl - slowly at first, then faster and faster. Spinning crazily like a huge runaway top, it darted up, down, and about the hillside.

Tom and his two companions stared in helpless amazement.

"Great horned toads! What's it up to?" Chow exclaimed.

"Seems like the energy's trying to get out!" Bud guessed. "Something must be bothering it."

Tom shook his head incredulously. "No reason for that. The container was absolutely empty."

Chow suddenly gave a groan and slapped his forehead in dismay. "Brand my Big Dipper!" the cook said. "Mebbe Ole Think Box has gone loco! An' it could be my fault!"

Victor Appleton

CHAPTER XI

AN ELECTRICAL CHRISTENING

"What are you talking about, Chow?" Tom asked, turning to the old Westerner in amazement.

Chow related how he had dropped the bubble gum inside the robot's head. "Did I ruin the critter?" he asked fearfully.

Tom was thoughtful for a moment, frowning as they watched Ole Think Box continue its gyrations. The figure seemed to be calming down somewhat, although Tom could not be sure of this.

Suddenly his face brightened. A new thought had just struck the young inventor! To Chow's amazement, Tom slapped the cook happily on the back.

"I think you've done me a favor, Chow!" he exclaimed.

"I have?" The old Texan stared at his young boss, as if not sure whether or not to believe him. "How come?"

"You saw how Ole Think Box reacted to the gum," Tom explained. "That shows the energy really is like a brain! It's responsive and sensitive to conditions of its environment, especially when coming up against something new and unexpected."

"You mean they don't have bubble gum on Planet X?" Chow asked with a grin.

Tom smiled as Bud said, "This means we should be able to communicate with it."

"And the brain will probably be able to communicate back to us!" Tom went on excitedly. "We may even be able to learn about Planet X!"

As he spoke, Ole Think Box's whirling became slower and slower. Finally it came to rest close to the three humans.

"What do you suppose happened to the gum?" Bud asked. "Did he chew it all up?"

"It's probably unchanged," Tom replied. "Our visitor is used to it now."

Chow was still wide-eyed with awe. He stared at the strange creature as if expecting it to snap at him in revenge for the gum.

"Don't worry, old-timer. Think Box won't bite," Bud teased. "With that gum spree, he's just been initiated into our American tribal customs!" The pilot grinned. "Hey! We haven't given him a proper name."

"You're right." Tom looked at his pal and chuckled. "Got any ideas?"

"Hmm. Let me see." Bud scowled and paced about with his hands clasped behind his back. "Firetop -

John Q. Pyro -"

"But it ain't on fire now," Chow pointed out.

"Maybe not, but he sure blazed a trail getting here," Bud argued.

Tom and Chow countered with several ideas of their own, but nothing seemed suitable until Bud suddenly stopped short and snapped his fingers.

"I have it! He's a visitor from Planet X, so let's call him *Exman!*" Bud spelled it out.

"Perfect!" Tom was delighted and Chow agreed that it seemed "a right good monicker." The Texan insisted seriously that if the creature were going to be named, he should also have a proper christening.

"Why not?" Tom agreed, as both boys broke into laughter. Bud also liked the idea.

Chow had a troublesome afterthought. He shoved back his sombrero, squinted frowningly at the brain container, and scratched his bald head. "For boat christenings and statues and what not, you break bottles on 'em or cut ribbons or pull a sheet off 'em," the cook said. "But how in tarnation do you christen a buckaroo from space?"

"Nothing to it, Chow," Tom assured him. "We'll do the job up nice and fancy with a display of electricity. But first let's get Exman over to the lab."

The three loaded the energy container into the pickup truck which had brought it to the hillside spot. Then

Tom drove back to Enterprises and they took Exman into his private laboratory.

Here Tom attached an electrode to each side of the star head. One electrode was safely grounded, the other connected to a Tesla coil. Then, with all lights turned off in the laboratory, Tom threw a switch.

Instantly a dazzling arc of electricity sputtered through the darkness across the creature's head! The eerie display lit up the room with such impressive effect that both Bud and Chow felt their spines tingle.

"I christen you Exman!" Tom intoned.

For several moments he allowed the fiery arc to continue playing about the star head. Then he opened the power switch and turned the room lights back on.

"Wow! Quite a ceremony!" Bud murmured.

"After a send-off like that, I'll be expectin' the critter to do great things here on this lil ole planet Earth!" Chow declared fervently.

"You could be right," Tom said.

Worn out by the long wait for their visitor from Planet X and the excitement following his arrival, Chow finally went off to his own quarters at Enterprises for a well-earned sleep.

"Guess you and I had better get some shut-eye too, pal," Tom told Bud. "And I think I won't tell Dad until morning."

The two boys decided to bunk on cots in the small apartment adjoining Tom's laboratory. Exman, meanwhile, was left locked in the laboratory with a tiny "night light" showing on him.

"Just a little ray of energy to keep him company," Tom explained with a chuckle.

Minutes later, the two boys were sound asleep. For a while, all was silent. Then the apartment's telephone rang, shattering the stillness. Tom struggled out of the depths of sleep, got up, and groped his way over to the wall phone.

"Tom Swift Jr. speaking."

A familiar voice asked, "Did it come?"

"Oh, hi, Dad!" Tom replied, yawning. "Yes, Exman arrived in fine shape. We've put him to bed. Tell you all about it tomorrow morning."

"Okay, Tom."

As Tom hung up, Bud roused and switched on a lamp. He had awakened in time to catch only part of Tom's words. "Your father?" he inquired.

Tom nodded sleepily and was about to go back to bed. But Bud, still fascinated by the space visitor, decided to have a peek at Exman. He got up and opened the door to the laboratory. A yell from him brought Tom rushing to his side.

"Hey! It's gone!"

The spot by the night light where they had left Exman was now deserted! Tom found a wall switch and pressed it. As light from the overhead fluorescent tubes flooded the room, the boys gave laughing cries of relief.

Ole Think Box had merely moved himself to another corner of the room!

"Guess he didn't like that little chum we left on for him," Bud said with a chuckle.

"Let's leave him where he is," Tom agreed.

The two boys went back to the adjoining apartment and were soon asleep again. Several hours later they were rudely awakened by a loud crash of glass and a heavy thud.

"Something's happening to Exman!" Tom cried.

With Bud at his heels, the young inventor dashed into the laboratory.

Victor Appleton

CHAPTER XII

EXMAN TAKES ORDERS

A strange sight greeted Tom's and Bud's eyes. In the first rays of sunlight, the space robot was moving back and forth about the laboratory in wild zigzag darts and lunges.

As he rolled toward a bench or other object, the brain energy seemed to send out invisible waves that knocked things over! Already the floor was strewn with toppled lab stools, books, and broken test tubes. The heavy thud had apparently been caused by a falling file cabinet.

"Stop him!" Bud yelped.

Exman was heading straight for a plate-glass window! Reaching from floor to ceiling, the glass formed one entire wall of the laboratory.

"Oh, no!" Tom tensed, realizing that it was hopeless to try to stop Exman in time.

But an instant later, the rolling robot stopped of its own accord, as if registering the fact that its energy waves were now striking a fragile surface. The thick pane of glass vibrated in its frame.

"Good grief!" Tom wiped his brow. "Let's corral that thing before he wrecks the whole lab!"

Exman was already rolling off on a new tack. The two boys managed to grab him before more harm was done. The brain energy in its container seemed to calm under their touch.

"What in the name of space science triggered it off?" Bud wondered out loud.

"Time. It must have reacted to the passage of time," Tom conjectured. "I suppose it just decided to explore this place." He added a bit nervously, "The sooner we can communicate with this energy, the better!"

"But how?" Bud asked.

Tom's brow furrowed. "Say, I wonder if Exman might understand a direct order?"

Tom backed a few paces away from the space robot, then said in a loud, clear voice, "Come here!"

Exman remained fixed to its spot.

"Move right!" No response. "Move left!" Still no response.

"Guess you're not getting through, skipper," Bud commented with a grin.

"No," Tom agreed. "I can't predict what kind of energy this brain will respond to. Being only energy, it must respond to other energy and sound is our form of energy. The problem is the same as with radio waves, which are also energy. We must figure out how we can vary the energy, so it can transmit information to Exman."

"What *do* we try?" Bud asked. "Or is it hopeless?"

"I'll try communicating with it via the electronic brain, which I have adapted to fit this problem."

The boys cleaned up the wreckage caused by Exman in his dawn venturings. Then Tom went by jeep to the computer laboratory, made connections to his electronic brain, and wired it for remote control. Then he returned to the private laboratory. There Bud watched as he hooked up the leads from the computer to a transmitting-receiving decoder with a short-range antenna.

"Speak, O Master!" Bud said, imitating a squeaky robot voice. "Sound off loud and clear!"

Tom grinned and tapped out a command on the keyboard: *Move backward.*

Exman rolled backward! Bud gave a whoop of delight.

Tom signaled: *Move forward.* Obediently Exman rolled toward him.

Stop. Exman stopped.

"Hey, how about that?" Bud exclaimed happily. "It really savvies those electronic brain impulses!"

"And minds them - which is equally important," Tom added.

A moment later the brain energy seemed to become impatient. It spurted off in its wheeled container toward a laboratory workbench.

Crash! A rack of test tubes went sailing to the floor with an explosion of tinkling glass.

Stop! Tom signaled frantically. Again Exman obeyed the order.

"It's like a mischievous kid," Bud said.

Almost as if in defiance, Exman scooted off in another direction. Then it stopped abruptly and swiveled around, one of its antenna arms nocking a Bunsen burner to the floor as it did so.

Come here! Tom signaled. As the culprit approached, he added sternly, Stop where you are. And stay there until you receive further orders.

This time Exman stood patiently, awaiting the next signal. Bud got a rush and dustpan, and the boys cleaned up the broken test tubes and eplaced the burner on its shelf.

Then Tom began feeding more complicated instructions to Exman through he electronic brain. He guided him through a number of dancelike ovements and other drills, and got him to send out a wave of heat which the boys could instantly feel. Tom was even able to make the robot aim its wave energy so as to short-circuit a switch on an electrical control panel.

Tom was both pleased and excited. "Bud," he exclaimed, "the brain reacts as quickly as that of a highly intelligent being! Just imagine - without any sort of decoding equipment, it can pick up and *understand* the radio signals I beam out to it!"

"What we need now," Tom went on, "is a simple language to get our ideas across to Exman without having to use the electronic brain all the time. That means I must find a way to give Exman senses as we humans have - smell, touch, sight, hearing, taste. Then it could receive the same reactions we do and talk directly to us!"

"Sounds like quite an order," Bud said wryly. "Speaking of which, how about us phoning Chow an order for breakfast?"

He did so, and a short time later Chow wheeled a food cart into the laboratory. As he dished out man-sized helpings of ham and eggs, the cook kept a wary eye on Exman. Tom was putting the robot through a few more lively maneuvers.

"A good meal'd calm down Ole Think Box," Chow observed grumpily. "But what do you feed that there kind o' contraption?"

"Well, not gum, that's for sure!" Bud teased. After tasting his first forkful of food, he gasped, "And none of this ham!"

Jumping up from his lab stool, Bud began whirling, dancing around, and flapping his arms as if he were burning up.

"Help! Help!" he yelled. "Chow's poisoned me - just like he did Exman!"

Chow's leathery old face paled under its desert tan. "Great snakes, Tom!" the Texan gulped. "Have I really pizened him? Maybe we should call Doc Simpson!"

Doc was the medic in charge of the Enterprises infirmary.

Tom was unable to keep a straight face. "Better call someone with a strait jacket - or a butterfly net!" he said, quaking with laughter. "I'm afraid he's just pulling your leg, Chow!"

Chow's jaw clamped shut like a bear trap and he glared at the pirouetting young flier. Bud collapsed on his stool, doubled over with mirth.

"Sorry, old-timer," he gasped. "I just couldn't resist!"

"Okay, Buddy boy," Chow said darkly. "And mebbe I won't be able to resist gettin' even one o' these days!" The cook stumped out of the laboratory in his high-heeled cowboy boots, a picture of outraged dignity.

"Better watch out, pal!" Tom warned with a grin. "Just remember: it's never smart to bite the hand that feeds you!"

"I guess you're right," Bud agreed, wiping away the tears of laughter. "I'll remember, just as long as Chow promises not to serve us any more armadillo soup or rattlesnake salad!"

Chow's fondness for experimenting with weird dishes was a standing joke around Enterprises.

The boys ate their meal hungrily. As they were

finishing, Tom glanced at the big clock on the wall. It was now well past eight o'clock.

"Wonder why Dad hasn't come to the lab," he remarked. "I'd better call and find out if he's all right."

Tom picked up the telephone and asked the operator for the direct line to the Swifts' home. His father answered.

"'Morning, Dad!" Tom greeted him. "I thought after your call last night, you'd be over bright and early to see our visitor. He's already -"

"What are you talking about, son?" Mr. Swift broke in. "I didn't phone you last night!"

CHAPTER XIII

DISASTER STRIKES

Tom was thunderstruck. "You didn't phone me? But, Dad, I got the call - I definitely heard your voice!"

"That's impossible," Mr. Swift insisted. "Believe me, son, I slept soundly from the time I turned in until a little while ago."

There was a moment of stunned silence as both Swifts realized that the telephone call had been faked! Then Tom exclaimed:

"Dad, this is serious!"

"Deadly serious, I agree," his father replied. "Are you calling from your lab?"

"Yes!"

"Stay there. I'll be right over," the elder scientist said.

When Mr. Swift arrived, Tom related his conversation with the mysterious caller. His father listened with worried eyes and a puzzled frown.

"It's bad enough that an enemy was able to get the

information," Mr. Swift remarked. "But, potentially at least, it's even more dangerous that he was able to imitate my voice so well. If he could fool you, Tom, he could fool anyone!"

"Are you thinking the same thing I am, Dad?"

"That it may have been some insider here at Enterprises?" When Tom nodded, his father gravely agreed. "Yes, son, it does look that way. To imitate my voice convincingly, it would almost certainly have to be someone who's had close contact with us - either at the plant or here in Shopton."

The thought of a traitor at the experimental station was repugnant to the Swifts and to Bud as well. Not only were all employees carefully screened, but there was a close, almost family relationship among those who took part in the exciting scientific ventures at Swift Enterprises.

Tom called Security and asked Harlan Ames to come over to the laboratory at once. The security chief arrived within moments. Quickly Tom filled him in on the details of the puzzling telephone call.

"Think back, skipper," Ames urged. "Was there anything at all you can remember about the voice that might give us a tip-off? I mean, was it deep, or maybe a bit higher-pitched than you expected? Or anything about the way the caller pronounced his words?"

Tom shook his head. "Nothing. That's the trouble. He spoke only a couple of sentences, but so far as I knew, it *was* my father calling!"

"Hmmm." Ames frowned. "What about background noises?"

Tom thought hard. "None. If I had detected any special sounds during the call, I'm sure they would have stuck in my mind."

Ames tried another tack. He asked how many people had known about the expected arrival of the brain energy from space. This was harder to answer, but as Tom and his father enumerated the persons, it did help to narrow the circle of suspects.

Besides the Swifts, Chow, Phyl, Ames, and George Dilling, there were three groups who had had access to the information. One was the radio operators at the space-communications laboratory. Another consisted of Arv Hanson and Hank Sterling and the workmen who had taken part in building the energy container. The last group, which also included Hank and Arv, were the technicians who had actually gone to the hillside to await the visitor from Planet X.

Tom scowled. "None of those people would pull such a trick, Harlan - any more than the ones like you and Arv and Hank who are above suspicion. Most of them could have easily obtained the news without going through such a rigmarole."

Mr. Swift nodded. "Tom's right. Unless, of course, they had some urgent reason for wanting to find out as soon as possible."

"Which makes me think it may have been an outsider after all," Tom argued. "Remember, the Brungarians may have intercepted the code messages to or from our space friends." After a moment's silence, he added gloomily, "Whoever the caller was, he knew the energy was arriving. And now he knows it's here!"

Bud interjected, "Well, if he was a Brungarian agent and he's hoping to steal the brain energy, one thing's sure. No earthquake will demolish this place as long as the energy is here at Enterprises."

"A comforting thought, Bud," Mr. Swift commented with a wry smile.

Again Tom frowned. "At any rate, Harlan, see if you can get a line on that impostor."

Ames departed to begin a thorough check of all personnel at the plant who might have been implicated. Bud went on an errand, as Tom began showing his father the accomplishments of the space robot.

"We've christened him Exman," Tom said.

By means of the electronic brain, he made the visitor do a number of maneuvers in response to orders.

"Wonderful!" Mr. Swift exclaimed, greatly impressed. "Let's see if he can use his caterpillar treads as well as he does the wheels."

Tom brought a small flight of portable aluminum stairs which he used for reaching up on high shelves or tinkering with outsized machines. Tom was uncertain at first how to code the command, having no symbol for steps or stairs. Finally he moved Exman to the bottom of the steps and signaled simply: *Go up!*

Exman paused for a moment, then attempted the ascent. His caterpillar tracks clawed their way up the first step. Then, gingerly, he essayed the next. The robot body tilted, but its gyro kept it from toppling over.

"Bravo!" Mr. Swift applauded encouragingly. But the next instant Exman gave up! He slid back to the floor again with a heavy bump. Then he began whirling and darting about madly.

"Good night! Exman's gone berserk!" Tom cried.

Now wafts of smoke could be seen issuing from the robot's wheels. He was banging wildly about the laboratory, leaving a trail of havoc.

Bud, who had returned, opened the door to come in. Instantly Exman lunged toward him, antennas sparking fiercely and wheels smoking. Bud slammed the door hastily.

The Swifts, too, found it wiser to take cover. They crouched behind a lab workbench until the frenzy was over. Presently Exman subsided and rolled to a complete standstill.

"Good grief!" Tom stood up cautiously and eyed the creature. It made no further move. Bud poked his head through the doorway for a wary look, then re-entered the laboratory.

"What made him blow his top?" Bud asked.

Then Tom heard a quiet chuckle from his father. "Actually, boys," the elder scientist said, "I think we should be encouraged."

"*Encouraged?*" Tom stared at his father.

Mr. Swift nodded. "Yes, the whole thing was rather a noteworthy reaction. I believe Exman was displaying a fear complex about navigating up those stairs."

Tom gasped, then broke out laughing. "Dad, you're right! I'll bet when its body tilted over, the brain wasn't sure whether the gyro would keep it from being wrecked. It just shows Ole Think Box is getting more human all the time!"

Bud ventured to pat Exman on its "back." "Relax, kid," he said with a chuckle. "You're among friends and we wouldn't dream of letting you get hurt. You're too valuable!"

Mr. Swift stroked his jaw thoughtfully. "Valuable, yes, if we can only get it to communicate. Tom, I believe the first project we should work on is a way to make Exman talk."

After the debris had been cleaned up, the two scientists pulled up stools to the workbench and began to discuss the problem. Bud, seeing them absorbed, and realizing the discussion would soon be far beyond his depth, snapped a grinning salute at Exman and quietly left the laboratory.

"Dad, the toughest part won't be the speech mechanism itself," Tom pointed out. "There are several ways we could handle that - by modulating a column of air, for instance, or by some sort of speaker diaphragm. The real stumper will be how to teach him our spoken language."

Mr. Swift nodded. "I'm afraid you're right. If the inhabitants of Planet X communicate telepathically, or by some sort of wave transfer, they may have long since forgotten any concept of a spoken language."

The Swifts batted several ideas back and forth. Then Tom snapped his fingers.

"Wait, Dad! We have the answer! The electronic brain!"

Mr. Swift's eyes lighted up. "Of course! The machine already translates the space code into written English. All we need do is add a device to convert the machine's impulses into sound!"

In two hours the Swifts had put together a mechanism designed to work through a tape recorder. This was hooked up to the electronic brain.

After recording for several moments, Tom reversed the tape and switched on the playback. A squeaky jumble of noises could be heard. But one word seemed to come through fairly distinctly. "Universe!"

"It's talking!" Tom cried out.

"Trying to, but not succeeding very well," Mr. Swift said.

Nevertheless, the two scientists were jubilant at this first breakthrough. Eagerly they began making adjustments - both on the electronic-brain hookup and the converter mechanism. Tom was just about to switch on the tape recorder again when the telephone rang.

The young inventor was annoyed at being interrupted at such a crucial moment, but picked up the phone. "Tom Swift Jr. speaking."

"You have an urgent call from Washington," the operator informed him. "Just a moment, please."

Bernt Ahlgren was calling from the Pentagon. The defense expert's voice was strained.

"Tom, there's just been another attempt to cause an earthquake here in Washington!"

Tom gasped. "What happened?"

"It failed, thanks to you. But Intelligence believes an attempt will be made on New York City very soon. We need your help to stop it. How near completion are the other shock deflectors?"

Before Tom could answer, he heard excited voices at the other end of the line. Then Ahlgren broke in again abruptly.

"A news flash, Tom! The Walling range-finder plant has been demolished by an earthquake!"

CHAPTER XIV

AIR-BORNE HIJACKERS

Mr. Swift, hearing Tom's dismayed reaction, rushed to the telephone.

"What's wrong, son?"

Tom clamped his hand over the mouthpiece and quickly gave his father the news of the destroyed range-finder plant. Then he spoke into the telephone.

"Bernt, we must prevent another disaster! Let me check with our construction company on the Quakelizors and I'll call you right back!"

"Right, Tom," Ahlgren agreed.

Both Tom and Mr. Swift were shocked by this latest blow of their enemies. Tom called Ned Newton at the Swift Construction Company at once and told him the news.

"How soon will the Quakelizors be ready, Uncle Ned?"

"They're finished, Tom. We're running a final inspection on them right now. We can have them ready to ship out by one o'clock."

Tom relayed word to the Pentagon. Bernt Ahlgren was greatly relieved. "By the way," Tom went on, "what about the sites? Have they been chosen yet?"

"Only tentatively," Ahlgren replied. "We wanted to get your opinion first."

One of the deflectors, Ahlgren felt, should be based in position to guard the New York and New England area, in view of Intelligence warnings about a probable attack on New York City. Another, in the Cumberland plateau region of Kentucky, could damp out shock waves threatening either the heavily industrialized Great Lakes area or any southern city.

As to the other three Quakelizors, Ahlgren suggested that one be installed on the West Coast, one in the Black Hills of South Dakota, and the third on the Atlantic island of San Rosario. This would protect both Latin-American allies and Caribbean defense bases of the United States.

Before deciding, Tom asked that Dr. Miles at the Bureau of Mines be circuited into the telephone conversation. Mr. Swift, too, joined in on another line. The four scientists discussed the problem and referred to geologic maps. Finally the exact sites were agreed upon.

"Dad, I'm going to deliver and install one of those Quakelizors myself," Tom declared, after the telephone conference ended. "Judging from that phone impostor last night, there's no telling what sort of trick our enemies may try next!"

Mr. Swift approved heartily. "Good idea, son. In the

meantime, I'll see what I can accomplish with Ole Think Box here."

Tom notified Uncle Ned of the delivery sites. He requested that because of the urgency of the situation, Swift planes transport the Quakelizors. Mr. Newton promised to have five cargo jets loaded and prepared for take-off from the construction company airfield.

Next, Tom turned to the job of rounding up flight crews. He decided that Hank Sterling, Arv Hanson, Art Wiltessa, and a crack Swift test pilot, Slim Davis, would each captain a plane.

Tom was just hanging up the telephone when Chow wheeled in a lunch cart, bearing sizzling servings of steak for the two Swifts.

"How's Ole Think Box comin' along?" Chow inquired.

"All right now, but he went berserk a while back," Tom replied with a chuckle.

Chow eyed the robot apprehensively and made a hasty exit. Both Tom Jr. and Tom Sr. were amused.

As they ate, the two scientists continued their discussion on how to equip Exman with senses and the power of speech. Several minutes later, when they were finishing dessert, Bud came into the laboratory.

"Tom, what's this about you hopping off somewhere to install a Quakelizor?" he asked anxiously.

"Don't worry, pal. I'll need my usual copilot," Tom said with a grin. "Just didn't have time to call you before lunch. We'll be flying down to a place called San Rosario in the Caribbean."

At one o'clock Tom briefed the flight crews and technicians. Slim was provided with three men who had worked on the original model of the quake deflector. After making sure that every man knew his job, Tom had the groups flown by helicopter over to the Swift Construction Company airfield.

Tom and Bud's cargo jet was the second to take off. On signal from the tower, the big workhorse thundered down the runway and soared off into the blue. Soon it was spearing southward above the waters of the Atlantic.

Presently Bud drew Tom's attention to some blurry specks of light on the radarscope. "Looks like a formation of planes, skipper."

Tom studied the blips for a while. "Guess you're right. It's sure not a flock of sea gulls!" The young inventor frowned.

"Worried, Tom?" Bud asked quietly.

Tom shrugged. "It could be a routine military flight."

He increased speed and climbed for altitude. But the blips on the radarscope showed that the planes were coming steadily closer. It was clear that they were targeting on the Swift cargo jet.

Tom switched on the radio. Presently a voice crackled over their headphones:

"Calling Swift jet!" The voice was heavily accented.

"Brungarians!" Bud muttered.

Tom made no reply to the radio challenge. Again came the voice:

"Calling Swift jet! Make emergency landing on the water!"

Tom's only response was a fresh burst of speed. Gunning the jet motors, he sent the big cargo ship arrowing forward at supersonic velocity.

"There they are!" Bud cried suddenly. He pointed to a cluster of silvery glints in the sky at seven o'clock.

Tom zoomed downward into a billowing cloud bank. It was a feeble hope and Tom knew it. His only real chance now was to outrun or outmaneuver the marauders.

The slim hope faded as they emerged from the cloud cover moments later. The enemy planes were not only still dogging them, but closing in rapidly. Sleek, needle-nosed attack ships, they appeared to have seaplane hulls.

"Wow! Those are new ones!" Bud gasped.

"Our last warning to Swift jet! Hit the water or be shot down!" came the enemy voice.

Tom raced along, his mind searching frantically for a method of escape.

Bud switched off radio power momentarily. "If we're going to be hijacked, skipper, let's ditch your invention before it's too late!"

Tom shook his head stubbornly. "Why should I let those pirates bulldoze us? Actually, I think they're after Exman!"

This last thought was a hunch that had just occurred to Tom. It was clear that their foe had learned about the arrival of the energy from space. "But so far," Tom reasoned, "there's no cause to suppose they know anything about the quake deflectors."

Stalling for time, Tom switched on the radio again and spoke into the mike. "Swift jet to attack planes. Our home base is picking up every word of your threats. Shoot us down and America will consider it an act of war!... Care to risk it?"

There was a moment's silence, then a reply. "War, you say? How can there be a question of war? War against whom? You do not even know our national identity!"

"Don't kid yourselves, mister!" Bud put in with a snarl. "We know, all right, and so does United States Intelligence!"

Tom decided to risk a blunt query, without actually giving away any facts, in case his hunch about the Brungarian's knowledge was wrong.

"There was a phone call to Swift Enterprises last night," he radioed. "We know it was a fake. We also know your agents are aware of our visitor.... Right?"

After a pause, the enemy spokesman replied, "Perhaps. If so, what then?"

"Just this," Tom radioed back. "If you're hoping to meet our visitor, you're out of luck. I'll give you my word for it. Do you think we'd risk such a valuable character in an unguarded crate like this?"

Tom and Bud looked at each other. Somehow, both boys felt instinctively that Tom's words had struck home. The enemy had certainly risen to the bait.

Finally came the reply. "You Swifts have a reputation for scrupulous honesty." There was a slight sneer in the speaker's voice as if he considered this a foolish weakness. "You give me your word of honor that this - er - character is not aboard?"

"I do!" Tom snapped. "And if you don't trust me, go ahead and risk a war!"

The boys waited breathlessly for the outcome of Tom's bold gamble. Soon they saw the result. The pursuing planes suddenly peeled off and sped away in the direction from which they had first appeared.

"Whew!" Bud wiped his hand across his face and drew it away moist with perspiration. "How do you like that?"

Tom chuckled with relief. "I like it fine, fly boy. But I was sure worried there for a while!"

Less than an hour later, the big cargo jet touched down at the San Rosario airport. An armed guard was on hand to greet the boys, under command of an officer named Captain Sanchez. He had brought along a work crew of soldiers and also a geology expert, Professor Leone, from the island's small technical school.

"I have selected a spot on the eastern shore of the island," the professor told Tom. He unrolled a map and explained the site.

"Excellent," Tom agreed.

The Quakelizor parts, communications equipment, and small atomic earth blaster were quickly unloaded and transported to the site by trucks. In three hours the installation was finished.

Tom, who spoke Spanish fairly well, explained to a small group of San Rosario military technicians how the quake deflector worked. He also detailed one of his own men to stay on as trouble shooter for the setup.

"And now," said Captain Sanchez, beaming, "we must relax and celebrate the friendship of our two countries."

Tom and Bud, though eager to get home, hesitated to hurt the friendly officer's feelings. They sat through a delicious meal, followed by numerous speeches. When his own turn to speak came, Tom used it to warn against possible sabotage attempts by the Brungarians. At last the boys were allowed to take off with their crew.

"Swell guys," Bud said, when the boys were airborne, "but a bit hard to break away from!"

Tom grinned, then became serious. "You know, Bud,"

he said thoughtfully, "those aerial hijackers gave me an idea."

"Let's have it, skipper."

"If only I could get Exman perfected so he would report back to me," Tom explained, "I could *let* him be kidnaped. Think what a wonderful 'inside man' he'd make in the enemy setup! He could tip us off to everything the Brungarians were doing!"

"Hey, that's neat!" Bud exclaimed, wide-eyed. "But how could you be sure those Brungarian rebel scientists wouldn't change him somehow? I mean they might brainwash him or something."

"It's a risk," Tom agreed. "But that's my problem - how to make a perfect spy out of him."

It was midnight when the cargo jet touched down on the Enterprises airfield. The boys slept soundly.

The next morning Tom reported to Mr. Swift and Harlan Ames the outcome of his trip to San Rosario, including the attack en route by unmarked sky raiders. He also privately told his father about his plan to use Exman as an electronic spy. Mr. Swift was enthusiastic.

The two scientists promptly set to work. Mr. Swift built two powerful but miniature radio sets; one for receiving, one for transmitting. Tom, meanwhile, was busy on another device, also highly miniaturized, combining features of both the electronic decoder and Tom's famous midget computers, known as Little Idiots.

Victor Appleton

With this equipment, Tom hoped, Exman would be able to monitor all communications at Brungarian rebel headquarters, then radio the information to Enterprises.

Chow brought lunch to the laboratory at noon, and Bud came in later. Both stayed to watch the outcome of the experiment. Hank Sterling and Arv Hanson joined the group.

By midafternoon the equipment was ready for a tryout. Tom opened Exman's star head, inserted the gear, and made the delicate wiring connections.

"So far, so good," the young inventor murmured, stepping back. "Now for the real test! Will Exman answer our questions?"

Tom walked over to the electronic decoder brain and began to tap out a message on the keyboard. The others waited in breathless suspense.

CHAPTER XV

KIDNAPED!

The message which Tom signaled in code over the
electronic brain said:

WE HAVE A DANGEROUS PLAN. IF PLAN
WORKS, YOU MAY BE EXPOSED TO
ENEMY TAMPERING. WILL THIS BE SAFE?
CAN YOU STAND THIS?

There was a tense pause. Then the signal bell rang on
the machine and the keys began to punch out a reply
on tape:

NO ONE CAN ALTER THIS BRAIN NOR CAN
THEY CHANGE ITS PURPOSE. THEY CAN
ONLY DESTROY THE ENERGY HOLDER.

As Tom finished reading the message aloud, Chow
gave a whoop of delightand the whole group burst into
spontaneous cheers.

"Terrific, skipper!" Bud exclaimed, clapping his pal on
the back. The others gathered around to add their
congratulations.

Mr. Swift, beaming with pride, gave Tom a quick

hand-squeeze. "It's an amazing achievement, son. And it may prove to be the key for unlocking the secrets of space, if and when we have time for some research after this crisis is over."

"I sure hope so, Dad," Tom murmured. Though jubilant, the young inventor realized that this was only the first step in his plan to checkmate the Brungarian rebels.

The real perils still lay ahead!

Tom called Harlan Ames and asked him to come to the laboratory for a conference. When the security chief arrived, he was as impressed as the others with the way Tom was able to communicate with Exman.

"The problem now," Tom said, "is how do we have him kidnaped?"

Chow, wary as a coyote, offered his opinion that the safest way would be merely to leave the space robot unguarded somewhere about the grounds of Enterprises.

Ames shook his head. "Too obvious. They'd suspect a trap." Tom agreed.

"Wal, then, how about truckin' him along the highway hereabouts, as if you all were sendin' him down to Washington?"

This, too, was vetoed on the grounds that a shrewd espionage agent would guess that such a valuable prize would never be entrusted to a slow and vulnerable method of transport.

"Then what about an air flight?" Hank Sterling suggested.

"Brand my six-guns, that'd be jest beggin' to git yourself shot down!" Chow fumed.

"Not if we used a plane like the *Sky Queen*, equipped with jet lifters," Hank argued. "If any hijack planes jumped us, they'd have to let us come down safely in order to get their hands on Exman. We could land on the water or just hover while they made the transfer."

"And after they had it safe aboard their own plane, they'd blast yours to smithereens!" Chow retorted.

Tom, too, thought a plane flight unwise, but for different reasons. It might look suspicious to the Brungarians after the Swifts had been warned by one aerial hijack attempt. Also, they might be deterred by fear of war, thinking that the United States Air Force would doubtless be alerted to the possibility of attack.

"So right," Ames agreed. After a thoughtful pause, he added, "Tom, what about transporting Exman by submarine? We know that every spy apparatus in this hemisphere is constantly trying to probe what goes on at Fearing Island, where our subs are based."

"No doubt about that," Tom conceded.

"So," Ames continued, "any move to Fearing would certainly make the Brungarian agents prick up their ears. Their own spy subs probably would come prowling around the island and detect the departure of a Swift sub. And they might feel that an undersea hijack attempt would be a fairly safe gamble."

The others looked thoughtful, then slowly nodded in agreement. Ames's reasoning sounded highly logical.

"Tom, you'll insist on going, I suppose," Mr. Swift said somberly.

"Of course, Dad. After all, the kidnap plan was my own idea," Tom replied. "Another thing I'll insist on is that you *don't* go. We have Mother and Sandy to think of, and it's not right that both of us risk our necks."

Realizing that it was hopeless to dissuade his son, and realizing the basic fairness of Tom's position, Mr. Swift did not argue. Bud, Hank, Chow, and Arv immediately volunteered to accompany the young inventor on his dangerous mission.

Tom gratefully accepted their help. He asked all hands to assemble on the Enterprises airfield at six the next morning for the flight to Fearing.

After the others had left, Tom and his father resumed their experiments with Exman. Mr. Swift suggested adding a device to the radio equipment to make it disintegrate if tampered with. "Before those rebel Brungarians can learn the secret of your electronic spy."

"Good idea, Dad. And how about our doing the job with Swiftonium?" This was an unusual radioactive ore which Tom had discovered in South America.

Mr. Swift nodded as he began work.

Tom watched admiringly as his father reconstructed the radio, coating the entire thing with a Swiftonium compound. He at once placed the set in a small oven which he raised to 50 degrees centigrade.

"When this cools, the set will be stable," Mr. Swift said. "But if you should move any part of it after it cools, all of the organic parts, like the circuit boards, the insulation, the carbon resistors, etc., will oxidize and disappear as gas. You will not even be able to tamper with a single unit."

"Wonderful, Dad," Tom murmured when the device was finished. "I wish I had your know-how in microchemistry."

"And I wish I had yours in electronics!" the elder scientist declared with a chuckle.

After Mr. Swift had installed the device in Exman's star head, Tom used the electronic brain to inform the robot about the whole scheme.

Both Tom Jr. and Tom Sr. were delighted when Exman showed real enthusiasm. It replied via the printed tape on the decoder:

> DO NOT WORRY, MY FRIENDS. I WILL NOT RESPOND TO ANY ATTEMPTS BY BRUNGA-RIAN SCIENTISTS TO COMMUNICATE WITH ME. MY PLANET IS WELL AWARE OF THEIR DANGEROUS AIMS. HAVING CONQUERED YOUR WORLD, THEY WOULD NEXT INVADE SPACE.

"Looks as though Exman's got their number, all right!" Tom said with satisfaction.

Early the next morning Mr. Swift drove Tom to the Enterprises airfield to meet his friends. Hank Sterling, Bud, and Chow were already on hand, and Arv Hanson arrived a few moments later. Tom and Bud left the others to bring Exman in a small panel truck.

Soon the space robot was safely loaded aboard a transport helicopter. The others took their places inside the cabin.

"Good luck, son!" Mr. Swift forced a smile as he gave Tom a parting handshake.

"Don't worry, Dad. I'll be back soon!" Tom assured him. The nature of the trip had been described only vaguely to Mrs. Swift and Sandy in order to keep them from worrying.

The short hop overwater to Fearing Island was soon completed. Lying just off the Atlantic coast, Fearing had once been a barren, thumb-shaped expanse of scrubgrass and sand dunes. Now it was the Swifts' top-secret rocket base, tightly guarded by drone planes and radar.

As the helicopter approached its destination, Tom radioed for clearance, then whirred down toward the landing field. The barracks, workshops, and launching area of the base lay spread out in full view. Cargo rockets bristled on their launching pads, along with Tom's spaceships, including the mighty *Titan*, and the oddly shaped *Challenger* and *Cosmic Sailer*.

North and south, the island was fringed with docks. Here the recovery tugs and fuel tankers were moored, as well as the Swifts' fleet of undersea craft.

Tom had chosen a cargo-hauling jetmarine, named the *Swiftsure*. It was a larger version of his original two-man jet sub, the *Ocean Dart*. He had given orders the night before to have it ready for sea by morning.

By jeep and truck, Tom's group sped across the island to the dock. Exman was quickly lowered aboard through the sub's hatch. The others followed, the conning-tower hatch was dogged shut, and soon the *Swiftsure* was gliding off into the shadowy blue-green depths.

"What's your sailing plan, skipper?" Hank Sterling inquired. The quiet-spoken, square-jawed engineer stood beside Tom at the atomic turbine controls and looked out through the transparent nose of the jetmarine.

"Go slow. Give 'em plenty of chance to pick up our trail," Tom replied.

For two hours they cruised at moderate speed. Nothing happened. Disappointed, Tom surfaced and radioed his father for news, after cutting in the automatic scrambling device.

"You're in time for an exciting flash," Mr. Swift reported jubilantly.

"What is it, Dad?"

"An attempt to earthquake New York has just failed!"

Grins broke out on the faces of the crew as they heard Mr. Swift's words come over the loud-speaker. Bud let out a happy whoop.

Victor Appleton

"That's great, Dad!" Tom said. "Maybe we've got 'em licked on the quake front. No luck so far, though, on our new project."

"Well, keep in touch and let me know at once if anything happens," Mr. Swift urged.

"Right, Dad!" Tom promised.

Again the *Swiftsure* submerged. This time it was only a few minutes before Arv Hanson gave a cry of warning.

"Something on the sonarscope, skipper!"

Bud, Hank, and Chow hastily gathered around the scope to watch. The blip grew larger rapidly. It was clearly another submarine, closing in on a collision course.

Tom put on a burst of speed, as if attempting to outrace their pursuer. But he was careful to gauge his knots by reports from the sonarscope, in order not to widen the gap between the two craft. There seemed no danger that this would happen, although the *Swiftsure* raced ahead faster and faster. Still the enemy sub continued to close in like a marauding shark, finally passing Tom's craft.

"Some baby!" Bud muttered respectfully.

The words were hardly out of his mouth when a missile streaked across their bow, in plain view through the *Swiftsure's* transparent nose. Its foaming wake rocked the jetmarine.

"They're attacking us!" Bud cried out.

Tom slammed shut the turbine throttle, bringing his craft to a gliding halt in the water. At the same time, he switched on the sonarphone.

"Orders to Swift sub!" a voice barked over the set. "Surface and heave to! No tricks, or the next missile will not be across your bow!"

Tom blew his tanks and sent the *Swiftsure* spearing upward. As the conning tower broke water, Tom and his men swarmed up on deck. Seconds later, a sleek gray enemy submarine knifed into view. Its hatch opened and several men climbed out.

To Tom's amazement, their leader was Samson Narko!

Chow let out a yelp of rage. "Why, you sneakin', double-dyed, bushwhackin' polecat!" the old Westerner bellowed. "We shoulda kept you hawg-tied, 'stead o' lettin' you go free!"

Narko ignored the outburst and raised a megaphone to his lips. "Hand over your cargo and do it quickly!"

"What cargo?" Tom snapped back. "And what's the meaning of this outrage? You realize this is piracy?"

"I realize you will wind up on the bottom at the slightest show of resistance!" Narko warned menacingly. "You know very well what cargo I refer to! Now do not try our patience!"

Tom and his crew pretended to put up a blustering, indignant front. Chow was especially convincing, with a blistering torrent of salty Texas invectives.

Narko's only response was a barked-out order to his men in Brungarian. Quickly the enemy submarine maneuvered closer until the two craft were almost chockablock. Narko and his men then leaped aboard the *Swiftsure*, armed with sub-machine guns and automatics.

"I'm warning you, Narko -" Tom began angrily. But Narko cut the young inventor short by a poke in his ribs with the gun muzzle, then issued orders to two of his men to go below.

Moments later, Exman was being hauled up through the hatch and transferred aboard the raider. The Americans glared in angry silence.

"Thanks so much, my stupid friends!" Narko taunted them with a jeering laugh. Then he followed his crewmen as the last one scrambled back to the enemy submarine.

With laughs and waves, they disappeared into its conning tower. The hatch was clamped shut and the raider promptly submerged.

Tom and his men were amazed, but delighted at not having been taken prisoner along with Exman. All of them broke into happy chuckles of relief.

"Wow! That's what I call fast service!" Bud exclaimed.

"It was sure a blamed sight easier'n I expected," Chow said. "Thought fer a while we might end up feedin' the fishes!"

"You put on a real act, Chow!" Tom said, clapping the

stout old cook on the back. "Well, they've taken the bait. Now let's hope it pays off - for us!"

The Americans swarmed below again, closed the hatch, and submerged. Tom took his time in bringing the jet pumps up to speed. "Wonder if we should pretend to proceed on course, or turn around and head for home?" he murmured to Hank.

Hank's reply was cut short by a yell from Hanson at the sonarphone.

"Missile coming, skipper! Straight at us!"

CHAPTER XVI

A UNIQUE EXPERIMENT

"Bearing?" Tom cried.

"One-seven-five!" Arv Hanson sang out.

Tom gunned his port jet turbine and swung the *Swiftsure* hard right. The abrupt turn at high speed sent the craft sideslipping crazily like a skidding race boat.

"Here she comes, skipper!" Bud yelled. He had rushed to the sonarscope with the other members of the crew.

Tom's maneuver had carried them a good hundred yards off the missile's course. Now he yanked a lever, pulling the cadmium rods still farther from the atomic pile, in order to increase power and jet-blast their sub still farther out of range.

But suddenly the men at the scope blanched. "The missile's turning too!" Hank cried. "It's homing in on us!"

Unlike most Swift craft used on scientific expeditions, the cargo sub's hull had not been coated with Tomasite. This would have insulated it from all magnetic effects or any form of pulse detection. Tom had chosen the

Swiftsure partly for this very reason, so that the Brungarian rebels could easily pick up its trail after leaving Fearing.

How ironic if his choice should prove fatal! As the thought flashed through Tom's brain, the missile came streaking into view through the sub's transparent nose.

By this time, Tom had flipped up the *Swiftsure's* diving planes. The craft plummeted deeper into the ocean depths.

"Brand my whale blubber, she's turnin' again!" Chow gulped. The missile's arc, as it veered around to follow, painted a streak of light on the sonarscope.

Anxious moments raced by while Tom steered their craft in a deadly game of tag with the sub-killer. Gradually the missile appeared to be losing momentum.

"It's slowing down, all right!" Arv called out.

In a few minutes the missile had lost so much way that Tom was easily able to outdistance it. The crew crowded to the scope, heaving sighs of relief. The missile, its velocity spent, sank harmlessly toward the bottom.

"Boy, what a close call!" Bud gasped weakly. "You played that thing like a toreador sidestepping a bull, Tom! Nice going!"

The others echoed Bud's sentiments, with fervent handshakes and backslaps for Tom's skillful evasive action.

"Jest the same," said Chow, "I'd sure like to make Narko an' them Brungarian hoss thieves dance a Texas jig with a little hot lead sprayed around their boot heels! Sneakin' bushwhackers! It's jest like I told Hank about his airplane scheme - they'd try to gun us down, like as not, soon as they got their hands on Exman!"

"I guess you had them figured right, Chow," Tom agreed wryly. "Well, at least we've lost their sub!"

The Brungarian raider was no longer visible even as a faint blip on their radarscope. Evidently Narko had thought the jetmarine a sure victim and headed back to his own base.

Nevertheless, Tom steered a wary zigzag course back to Fearing. When they arrived at the island, he immediately telephoned Bernt Ahlgren and Wes Norris in Washington to report the hijacking of the space brain. Both men praised the young inventor for his daring scheme to outwit the ruthless Brungarian rebel clique.

"If your idea pays off, Tom, we should be able to checkmate every move those phonies and their allies make!" Norris declared.

"I'm hoping we can do even better than that," Tom replied. "Part of my plan is to help the Brungarian loyalists through Exman's tip-offs. With some smart quarterbacking, we might be able to rally the rightful government before all resistance is crushed out."

"Terrific!" Norris exclaimed. "Let's hope your scheme works!"

Tom had ordered the space oscilloscopes to be manned constantly, both at Fearing and at Enterprises, in case of a flash from Exman. But no word had yet been received when Tom and his companions arrived at the mainland late that afternoon.

Mr. Swift greeted his son warmly at the airfield. Tom had refrained from radioing the news to Enterprises after the hijacking and the missile attempt. Any such message, Tom feared, might be picked up by the enemy and bring on another attack. But the young inventor had telephoned his father immediately after calling Washington.

Now Mr. Swift threw his arm affectionately around the lanky youth. "You look pretty well bushed, son. Why not hustle home and call it a day? That goes for the rest of you, too," he added to Bud, Chow, and the others. "You've just risked your lives and the strain is bound to tell."

Tom urged his companions to comply. "But I'm sticking right here," the young inventor told his father. "I want to be on hand the minute Exman contacts us."

Bud insisted upon staying with his pal. The two boys ate a quiet supper in Tom's private laboratory and finally lay down on cots in the adjoining apartment. But first Tom posted a night operator to watch the electronic brain.

"Wake me up the second that alarm bell goes off," he ordered.

"Okay, skipper," the radioman promised.

No message arrived to disturb the boys' rest. Tom felt a pang of worry as he dressed the next morning, and then relieved the man on duty at the decoder. Had the Brungarians somehow outwitted him? Surely Exman should have reported by this time!

"Relax, pal," Bud urged. "Our space chum's hardly had time to learn any secrets yet. Besides, those Brungarian scientists are probably giving him the once-over with all sorts of electronic doodads. Why risk sending a message till he has something important to tell us?"

"That's true," Tom admitted.

Chow brought in breakfast. "You jest tie into these vittles, boss, an' stop frettin'," the cook said soothingly. "I reckon Ole Think Box won't let us down."

Tom sniffed the appetizing aroma of flapjacks and sausages. "Guess you're right, Chow," he said with a chuckle.

As the boys ate hungrily, Tom's thoughts turned back to the problem of how to equip Exman with senses. He talked the project over with Bud. Most of his ideas were too technical for Bud to follow, but he listened attentively. He knew the young inventor found it helpful to have a "sounding board" for his ideas.

"Too bad I didn't have time to tackle the job before Exman was kidnaped," Tom mused. "Think how much more he could learn with 'eyes' and 'ears'!"

"Stop crabbing," Bud joked. "Isn't an electronic spy with a brain like Einstein's good enough?"

Mr. Swift arrived at the laboratory an hour or so later. He found Tom setting up an experiment with a glass sphere to which were affixed six powerful electromagnets. Two shiny electrodes, with cables attached to their outer ends, had also been molded into the glass. Bud was looking on, wide-eyed.

Tom explained to his father that he had blown the sphere himself, following a formula adapted from the quartz glass used for view panels in his space and undersea craft.

"What's it for, son?" Mr. Swift asked, after studying the setup curiously.

"Don't laugh, Dad, but I'm trying to produce a brain of pure energy. A substitute for Exman, so we can go ahead with our sensing experiments."

Mr. Swift reacted with keen interest and offered to help. "But remember, son," he cautioned, "at best you can only hope to produce an ersatz brain energy - which will be vastly different from the real thing. Don't forget, Tom, the mind of a human being or any thinking inhabitant of our universe is based on a divine soul. No scientist must ever delude himself into thinking he can copy the work of our Creator."

"I know that, Dad," Tom said soberly. "Man's work will always be a crude groping, compared to the miracles of Nature. All I'm hoping to come up with here is a sort of stimulus-response unit that we can use for testing any sensing apparatus we devise."

The two scientists plunged into work. First, a bank of delicate gauges was assembled to record precisely every electrical reaction that took place inside the sphere. Then Tom threw a switch, shooting a powerful bolt of current across the electrodes. The field strength of the electromagnets, controlled by rheostats, instantly shaped the charge into a glowing ball of fire!

"Wow! A real hothead!" Bud wisecracked, trying to hide his excitement.

Tom grinned as he twirled several knobs and checked the gauges. The slightest variation in field strength triggered an instant response from the ball of energy. Mr. Swift tried exposing it to radio and repelatron waves. Each time the gauges showed a sensitive reaction.

"Looks as if we're in business, Dad!" Tom said jubilantly.

Bud left soon afterward as the two Swifts buckled down to work on the problem of perfecting an apparatus to simulate the human senses. Each concentrated on a different line of approach.

At noon they broke off briefly for a lunch wheeled in by Chow. Then silence settled again over the laboratory.

Tom had rigged up a jointed, clawlike mechanical arrangement with sensitive diaphragms in its "finger tips." The diaphragms were connected to a transistorized circuit designed to modulate the field current to the electromagnets.

Suddenly the young inventor looked up at his father with a glow of triumph.

"Dad, I just got a reaction to my sense-of-touch experiment!"

CHAPTER XVII

AN URGENT WARNING

Mr. Swift looked on eagerly as Tom explained and demonstrated his touch apparatus. By moving a pantograph control, Tom was able to manipulate the claws like a hand with fingers. Whenever they touched any material, the brain gauges instantly registered an electrical reaction inside the sphere.

The swing of a voltmeter needle showed how firmly the substance resisted the claw's touch, thus indicating its hardness or softness.

"With a computer device, such as we planted in Exman," Tom went on, "the brain would also be able to assimilate the textural pattern of any substance."

"Wonderful, son!" Mr. Swift exclaimed. "I hope I can do as well with this artificial sense of sight I'm working on."

Another hour went by before Mr. Swift was ready to test his own arrangement.

"You've probably heard of the experiments conducted with blind persons," he told Tom. "By stimulating the right part of their brain with a lead from a cathode-ray-tube device, an awareness of light and dark can be restored."

Tom nodded.

"Well, I'm using the same principle," Mr. Swift went on, "but with a sort of television camera scanning setup."

He asked Tom to draw the drapes and shut off the room lights, throwing the laboratory into complete darkness, except for the weirdly glowing "brain" in the glass sphere. Then Mr. Swift shone a flashlight at the scanner. The brain responded by glowing more brightly itself!

Next, after the drapes were opened again and the overhead fluorescent lights switched on, Mr. Swift painted a pattern of black-and-white stripes on a large piece of cardboard. He held this up to the scanner.

Visible ripples of brightness and less-brightness passed through the glowing ball of energy inside the sphere. It was reproducing the striped pattern!

"Dad, that's amazing!" Tom said with real admiration.

Mr. Swift shook his head. "Pretty crude, I'm afraid. The brain energy by itself can't take the place of a picture tube in a TV receiver. What we need an analog computer to sum up the scanning pattern picked up by the camera tube and then pass this information along in code form."

Before Tom could comment, the alarm bell rang on the electronic brain. The Swifts dropped everything and rushed to the machine.

"Wonder if it's Exman?" Tom exclaimed.

The answer was quickly revealed as the keys began punching out the incoming message on tape. At the same time, a flow of strange mathematical symbols flashed, one after another, on the lighted oscilloscope screen mounted above the keyboard.

Tom and his father read the tape as it unreeled.

> SPACE BEINGS TO SWIFTS. REQUEST INFORMATION ON PROGRESS AND RESULTS OF ENERGY SENT TO YOUR PLANET.

After a quick consultation with his father, Tom beamed out the reply:

> WE ARE PLEASED WITH RESULTS SO FAR. FURTHER EXPERIMENTS NOW GOING ON. REQUEST VISIT TO CONTINUE LONGER THAN TWENTY-ONE DAYS AS PLANNED.

Hopefully the Swifts stood by the machine. Would their space friends agree? As the minutes went by without a response coming through, father and son exchanged anxious glances.

"They've *got* to let Exman stay, Dad!" Tom said.

Mr. Swift nodded. "I'm afraid, though, the space beings have decided otherwise. They -"

He was interrupted by the ringing of the alarm bell.

"Message, Dad!" Tom said tersely.

A moment later they were overjoyed to see three words appear on the tape:

VISIT EXTENSION GRANTED.

Relieved, the two scientists went back to work on their sensing experiments. Twenty minutes later the signal bell rang again on the electronic brain.

"This time it *must* be Exman!" Tom cried.

The unreeling tape quickly bore out his guess.

EXMAN TO SWIFTS. TWENTY-FOUR-HOUR EARTHQUAKE UNDER HIGH LOYALTY.

"What!" Tom stared at the tape, his brow creased in a puzzled frown. "That 'twenty-four-hour earthquake' bit must mean he's warning us that a quake will occur in twenty-four hours. But what about the rest of it?"

"Hmm... 'Under high loyalty.'" Mr. Swift was as baffled as Tom. He studied the message for several minutes. It seemed highly unlikely that the electronic brain had made an error in decoding. Any new or untranslatable symbol caused a red light to flash on the machine.

"I think the only thing we can do is signal Exman and ask for a clarification, Tom," Mr. Swift decided at last.

Tom agreed. He beamed out a hasty code signal:

EXPLAIN MESSAGE.

Seconds later came Exman's reply. It was identical with the first message:

TWENTY-FOUR-HOUR EARTHQUAKE UNDER HIGH LOYALTY.

Tom and Mr. Swift stared at each other anxiously.

"Good night, Dad! This is horrible!" Tom exclaimed. "Exman sends us ample warning of a disaster and we're stymied!"

"Hi! What's going on, you two?" asked a merry voice. "More heavy thinking?"

Sandy Swift stood smiling in the doorway. The smile gave way to a look of concern as Tom explained the crisis.

"How dreadful!" Sandy gasped. "We *must* figure out what it means!... Wait a minute!"

Tom looked at her expectantly. "Got an idea, Sis?"

"Well..." The pretty, blond teen-ager hesitated. "You don't suppose Exman might have been translating some foreign words with a meaning similar to 'high loyalty'? For instance, high loyalty could mean 'good faith.' I know that in Latin 'good faith' would be *bona fide*."

"Sandy! You've guessed it!" Tom crossed the room in a single bound, gave his sister a quick hug, and whirled her around. "Exman must mean the Bona Fide Submarine Building Corporation! He didn't dare risk telling us the exact translation."

"Of course!" Mr. Swift was equally jubilant. But his face was grave as he added, "The company's located on the West Coast close to the San Andreas fault. Tom, a quake in that area could be devastating!"

"You're right, Dad," the young inventor replied. "I'll call Dr. Miles and Bernt Ahlgren at once!"

The telephone conversation that followed was grim with tension. Both government men begged Tom to take personal charge of the quake-deflection measures. Dr. Miles pointed out that tremors along the fault might trigger off a chain of quakes amounting to a national disaster.

After a hasty discussion, Tom agreed that he should station himself at the Colorado site, rather than at the West Coast Quakelizor installation. This would give him broader scope for damping out shock waves across the continent.

"I'll fly out immediately!" the young inventor promised.

Ahlgren, meanwhile, would flash orders to the Bona Fide Company and to civilian officials to have the entire area evacuated as soon as possible.

Hasty preparations were made for Tom's departure. He telephoned the airfield to have a jet plane with lifters readied for take-off. He also had Bud paged over the plant intercom. The copilot came on the run. When he heard the news, he was eager to accompany his pal.

"Listen, you two! I insist you have something to eat before you leave!" Sandy declared.

Victor Appleton

Tom was impatient over any delay. When Sandy proceeded to call Chow, the old Texan solved the problem by volunteering to go along as cook.

A short time later Chow came jouncing out to the airfield astride a motor scooter, hauling a cart loaded with supplies.

"Good grief!" Tom said, unable to suppress a grin. "We'll be back tomorrow, unless something goes wrong!"

"Bring food - that's my motto," Chow retorted, "like any good cook."

Minutes later, after a parting handshake from his father and a worried kiss from Sandy, Tom sent the sleek jet racing down the runway for take-off. Soon they were air-borne and heading westward. Chow served a tasty meal en route.

It was still daylight when the jet landed vertically in the Colorado canyon. The government crew manning the installation, and the Swift technician who had relieved Art Wiltessa as trouble shooter on the setup, greeted them eagerly.

"Looks as if we're in for a real test, Tom," said Mike Burrows, the engineer in charge.

"Let's hope we pass!" said Tom, holding up crossed fingers.

He checked every detail of the Quakelizor, power plant, and the communications gear. He opened an inspection panel in each of the dual-control spheres and tuned the kinetic-hydraulic units so as to step up the working pressure of the four powerful drivers.

"Well, all we can do now is wait," the young inventor muttered, wiping his arm across his forehead.

Tom passed the night in a fitful sleep, half expecting to be wakened at any moment by the stand-by crew on watch. No alarm occurred, however.

Dawn broke, and Chow delighted all hands with a hearty breakfast of bacon, eggs, and corn fritters. More hours of waiting dragged by.

"What time do you think the attack will occur?" Bud asked.

Tom shrugged. "The 'twenty-four-hour' business may have been approximate. But I'd say from two o'clock on is the danger period."

The young inventor checked frequently with Washington and the other crews stationed around the country. Suddenly the radiotelephone operator gave a yell.

"Your father is on the line, skipper!"

The scientist was calling from the receiver-computer headquarters at Enterprises. "Exman has reported a quake pulse will be sent in seven minutes - at 21.36 G.M.T."

"I'm ready, Dad," Tom said, then asked for various technical details before hanging up.

He passed the word to the crew and glanced at his watch. A hasty, last-moment inspection was carried out, every man checking certain details of the setup.

Soon the pulsemakers began ticking inside the dual-control spheres as they picked up the frequency signal by radio. Tom studied the gauge dials.

Tension mounted rapidly among the waiting group. The same thought was throbbing through every mind:

Was the nation on the brink of a terrible disaster? Or would Tom Swift's invention safeguard the threatened area?

As the deadline approached, Tom pushed a button. The mighty hydraulic drivers throbbed into action, sending out their pulse waves across the continent!

CHAPTER XVIII

EARTHQUAKE ISLAND

Now came the hardest part of all for Tom and his companions - waiting tolearn if the shock deflectors had succeeded in blotting out the enemy quake wave.

No one spoke. As the silence deepened inside the cave, the suspense became almost unbearable. Minutes passed.

"When will we know, skipper?" a crewman ventured at last.

"Soon, I hope," Tom replied tersely.

But the waiting seemed endless. Bud's eyes met Tom's. The flier grinned and held up crossed fingers, just as Tom had done to Mike Burrows the previous evening. Tom managed a feeble grin in response.

Suddenly the telephone shrilled, shattering the silence of the cave. Tom snatched it from the radioman's hands.

"Tom Swift here!... Yes?... Thank heavens! I guess we can all be grateful, Dr. Miles!"

"Providence protected us, I'm sure, Tom," the seismologist replied at the other end of the line. "But in this instance it worked through Tom Swift's Quakelizors! The Bona Fide plant and the surrounding area never even felt the tremor - your quake deflectors worked perfectly!"

There was no need to tell the others. Tom's words on the telephone and the grin on his face told the story. A spontaneous volley of cheers echoed through the cave as he hung up. Then the crew crowded around to slap Tom on the back and shake his hand.

"I hope the whole country learns what you've done, Tom," Mike Burrows said. "If it doesn't, I'll be the first to spread the word as soon as the secrecy lid's taken off!"

"Shucks, I knew all along Tom's contraption would do the trick!" Chow boasted, glowing with pride over his young boss's achievement.

Tom could only smile happily. "Guess we can go home now," he said to Bud and Chow.

They were preparing to leave when another flash from Washington came over the radiotelephone. A ship's captain, five hundred miles out on the Pacific, had just reported sighting a great waterspout, accompanied by considerable wave turbulence.

"It could have been the spot where the enemy shock waves and our deflector waves met and damped out," Tom commented.

"Dr. Miles thinks so, too," the caller said.

Soon the sleek Swift jet was arrowing back across the continent. En route, Tom radioed word of his latest triumph to Mr. Swift. As always, he used the automatic scramblers to make sure any enemy eavesdroppers would pick up only static.

"Great work, son!" Mr. Swift congratulated Tom. "I was confident you could handle the situation with your Quakelizors."

"Thanks, Dad. See you soon."

When the jet finally landed at Enterprises and came to a halt on the runway, the control tower operator spoke over the radio.

"Harlan Ames would like to see Tom Jr. at the security building. He left word just a few minutes ago."

"Roger!" Tom replied.

Chow frugally carted off his leftover supplies. Tom and Bud, meanwhile, went by jeep across the plant grounds to security headquarters.

Ames greeted the two boys enthusiastically. "Nice going on that earthquake situation, Tom!" he said. "And now I have some more good news. We've just nabbed the man who imitated your father's voice over the phone the other night."

"What!" Both boys were excited, and Tom added eagerly, "Who is he?"

"An actor at the Shopton summer playhouse."

"How did you find out?" Tom asked.

"I had a hunch," Ames went on. "If the impersonator wasn't a plant employee at Enterprises, then he had to be a person with a trained voice. That gave me the idea of checking on all actors and station announcers here in the vicinity. It paid off right away. The guy's name is Brent Nolan."

"Have you questioned him yet?" Tom asked.

"I'm about to," Ames replied. "Radnor just brought him in."

The security chief led the way into an adjoining office. A slender, good-looking young man with blond wavy hair was seated on a chair with Phil Radnor on one side of him and a Shopton police officer on the other. The actor was visibly nervous and perspiring.

"This is Tom Swift Jr.," Ames told him. "Brent Nolan."

Nolan nodded. "Yes, I've seen your picture in the papers many times." The actor tried to force a smile but his face muscles twitched. "I - I seem to have pulled a pretty dumb stunt by faking that phone call from your father. I'm sorry."

"What was the reason?" Tom asked.

Nolan fingered his wavy blond hair uneasily and swallowed hard. "A man named Professor Runkle paid me to do it."

"Professor Runkle?" Tom frowned. The name seemed

vaguely familiar.

"He spoke with a foreign accent. Said he was doing research at Grandyke University," Nolan explained. "He told me you might be expecting a rare biological specimen from the East Indies. He said both of you were eager to get hold of it for research purposes, but he was afraid that you had outbid him. However, if he asked you straight out, you would guard the secret very jealously. So he hired me to find out."

"Didn't it occur to you he might be an espionage agent?" Ames asked coldly.

Nolan seemed shocked. "Believe me, I had no such idea!" he averred. "Runkle seemed pleasant. He said it all was merely a short cut to save him from wasting any more time on the project. If Tom Swift had the specimen, he would quit. I - I guess I'm a little bit vain about the way I can mimic voices, and this gave me a chance to show off. Besides, I saw no harm in doing it."

"No harm?" Bud snorted. "You had Swift Enterprises in a real lather when we found out."

Nolan spread his hands in a helpless gesture. "I'm truly sorry," he repeated.

"How were you able to find out how my father's voice sounded?" Tom asked.

"I listened to a recording of a speech he made at the Fourth of July rally here in Shopton," Nolan explained. "I borrowed the tape from a local radio station. Guess that's how your security men got onto me."

"What did this fellow Runkle look like?" Ames asked.

Nolan thought for a moment. "Oh, he was past middle age, I should say. Grizzled hair, thick-lensed glasses. And he was quite heavy-set."

"Hmm. Then it certainly wasn't Narko," Ames murmured to Tom.

The young inventor nodded. "I believe I know him. The name just came back to me. I met a Professor Runkle in New York about a month ago, at a scientific convention. He was a member of the visiting Brungarian delegation."

"We'll check on him," Ames promised. He turned back sternly to the young actor. "All right, Nolan, I guess you can go. But I warn you - no more impersonations."

After more flustered apologies, the actor hurried out, obviously relieved.

"What a dumb egg he is!" Bud muttered.

"In a way he may have helped us," Tom pointed out. "If the Brungarian rebels hadn't found out about Exman, we couldn't have lured them into that kidnap plot. It's already helped us to save the Bona Fide Submarine Building Corporation."

Monday morning Ames reported that Professor Runkle had left the country. Tom was not sorry, since an arrest and public trial might have led to dangerous publicity about Exman. The probings of a sharp-tongued defense attorney might even have tipped off the Brungarian to Tom's real purpose in letting the space brain be hijacked.

Meanwhile, a telephone call from Washington announced that State Department men were flying to Enterprises to confer with the Swifts about taking official action against the Brungarian attacks. The group arrived by jet after lunch. Thurston of the CIA was also present.

"The problem is this," a State Department official said as they discussed the matter in the Swifts' office. "Should we bring charges against Brungaria before the United Nations? Or should we rely on other means, short of war, to block the Brungarian rebel coup?"

Mr. Swift frowned thoughtfully. "It might be difficult to prove they were responsible for the earthquake attacks," he pointed out.

"I'd say it's impossible," Tom said, "unless we give away the secret about our electronic spy." He paused, then added, "Sir, if the State Department will agree, I'd like more time before you make any official moves."

The Quakelizors, Tom argued, seemed to offer protection against any future quake waves, unless the power of the shocks was greatly stepped up. Meantime, working through Exman, Tom might be able to provide the Brungarian loyalists with valuable information. "I'm hoping it will help them overthrow the rebel clique and their brutal allied military bosses."

The State Department men conferred, then Thurston spoke up quietly, "In our opinion, it's worth a gamble."

After the group had left, the Swifts resumed their

sensing experiments in Tom's private laboratory. They were hard at work when the signal bell suddenly rang on the electronic brain.

The two scientists rushed to read the incoming message. It said:

EXMAN TO SWIFTS. ONE ENEMY EARTH-QUAKE PRODUCER IS AT...

Here the message gave precise latitude and longitude figures. It went on:

RUIN OF SWIFT PLACE IN ONE WEEK.

Tom and his father gasped in dismay. "I thought the New York-New England Quakelizor was going to protect us!" the young inventor exclaimed. "Our enemies must have located another earth fault with Enterprises right in its path!"

Hastily opening an atlas, Tom fingered the location of the proposed source of attack. It was Balala Island off the coast of Peru.

"Dad, that settles it!" Tom declared grimly. "It's clear now that those Brungarian rebels want to destroy us and use Exman in some way to conquer the earth!"

"I don't doubt that you're right, son," Mr. Swift said grimly. "We must act fast! But how?"

Again, the signal bell interrupted. This time, Exman gave a number of military details, evidently picked up from orders issuing from Brungarian rebel head-quarters. They concerned incoming troop movements from the north and operational plans for crushing out the last pockets of resistance by loyal government forces.

Tom recorded them with TV tape, then snatched up the telephone and called the Central Intelligence Agency in Washington. He relayed the information from Exman and asked if American agents could transmit it to the loyalists.

"Don't worry. Well see that it reaches them," the CIA chief assured Tom. "Many thanks. This *could* have important consequences."

As Tom hung up he decided on a bold move. "Dad, I'm going to lead a raid on Balala!"

"A raid!" The elder scientist was electrified.

"According to the atlas, the island is barren and deserted," Tom said, "so no friendly power will object if we land there. If it's being used as an enemy base for quake attacks against our country, we have every right to investigate. I might be able to learn the secret of the setup - perhaps even put the equipment out of commission."

"Nevertheless, a raid by a United States force could lead to trouble if the base there puts up any resistance," Mr. Swift said gravely.

"That's why I intend to handle it myself," Tom declared. "I'll take all responsibility."

Tom Sr.'s eyes flashed as he recalled some of his own hair-raising exploits in younger days. "All right, son," he said, putting a hand on Tom's shoulder. "I know I can trust your judgment. Good luck!"

Again Tom issued a call for volunteers. Bud, Hank Sterling, Arv Hanson, and Chow were all eager to take part. Within an hour they were taking off for Fearing. At the rocket base, they embarked in the *Sea Hound*, Tom's favorite model of his diving seacopter. A powerful central rotor with reversible-pitch blades, spun by atomic turbines, enabled the craft to rise through the air or descend into the deepest abysses of the ocean. Propulsion jets gave it high speed in either medium.

Loaded with equipment, the *Sea Hound* streaked southward through the skies - first to Florida, then across the Gulf and Central America into the Pacific. Here Tom eased down to the surface of the water and submerged.

It was near midnight when the *Sea Hound* rose from the depths just off Balala. The lonely rocky island lay outlined like a huddled black mass against the star-flecked southern sky. No glimmer of light showed anywhere ashore.

"Maybe no one's here," Bud murmured.

"Don't bank on that," Tom said. "They wouldn't be apt to advertise their presence to passing ships or planes."

Tom nosed inshore as closely as he dared from sonar soundings, finally easing the *Sea Hound* up to a rocky reef that fingered out from the beach. Then he, Bud, Hank, and Arv clambered out, armed with wrecking tools and powerful flashlights.

Chow, in spite of his muttered grumblings, was ordered to stay aboard and guard the ship with the other two crewmen who had come along.

Tom led his party cautiously ashore from the reef. They probed the darkness of the beach. Their footfalls sounded eerily in the night silence, broken only by the soughing of the sea wind and splash of breakers.

"Good place for spooks!" Bud whispered jokingly.

A steep draw led upward among the rocky slopes. A hundred feet on, Tom's group found the black yawning mouth of a cave. The yellow beams of their flashlights revealed a tunnel leading downward inside. Tom checked with a pocket detector. Its gauge needle showed no field force caused by electrical equipment in operation.

"Okay, let's go in!" Tom murmured.

Cautiously they moved into the tunnel. Then suddenly ahead of them a powerful dazzling light burst on, nearly blinding the searchers!

CHAPTER XIX

A FIENDISH MACHINE

A chill of fear gripped Tom and his companions as they blinked helplessly in the glare! Had the enemy detected them the first moment they had set foot on Balala Island? Had they walked blindly into a trap?

Gradually Tom's eyes and those of his friends adjusted to the dazzling radiance. A door, blocking the tunnel just ahead, had slid open and the light was pouring out of a room beyond.

"What happened?" Arv gasped.

Tom pointed downward to a pedallike plunger inserted in the tunnel floor. "This must be a switch," he explained. "When I stepped on it accidentally, it must have opened the door and flashed on the lights."

Bud whistled. "Wow! Let's be thankful it wasn't a booby trap!"

"Maybe it is," murmured Hank grimly.

Steeling their nerves, and with every sense alert, the searchers advanced into the secret room.

Tom suddenly gave a cry of amazement. "The earthquake machine!"

A huge hydraulic device, with massive steel bed and supporting pillars, looking somewhat like the enormous body presses found in automobile plants, stood embedded in a recess in one wall.

Tom rushed to the machine and examined it in fascination. A powerful diesel generator stood nearby with banks of complicated electrical equipment, amid a spider-web tangle of wiring. Tom assumed this gear was for timing and synchronizing the shock waves. Evidently the whole setup was operated from a single control panel in the wall, studded with knobs and dials.

"What a job of design!" Tom exclaimed in awe. His eyes roved over every detail of the equipment while he poked here and there with his hands. He was getting the "feel" of the setup almost as much by touch and handling as by his superb technical intuition. "Boy, I hate to admire anything those Brungarian rebel scientists do, but this is really masterful!"

"Yes? Well, don't go ga-ga over it," said Bud. "Let's do what we came to do and scram out of here. This place makes me jumpy!"

Tom appeared oblivious. "It seems like vandalism to wreck such an engineering achievement! Also, and this may sound strange to you," he went on in a doubtful tone, "are we *really* justified in taking the law into our own hands?"

"They're trying to wreck *our* setup, aren't they?" Bud retorted. "Think of the destruction they've caused already! Do you want to stand by and see Enterprises destroyed too?"

"Bud's right," Hank Sterling spoke up quietly. "Take a look at this."

He beckoned them over to another corner of the cave and pointed to a series of notations, crudely scrawled in white chalk on the cave wall. Half hidden behind a clump of rock, they would have escaped casual notice.

Tom read them and gave an angry gasp. A list of places and dates, already checked off, showed the quakes that had occurred so far. The last notation, not yet checked, said: SWIFT ENTERPRISES and was dated five days ahead.

"Okay, that's all the convincing I need!" Tom said grimly.

He issued quick orders. Hank and Arv were to rush back to the *Sea Hound*, get an underwater pump from the gear carried aboard, and install it just off the beach. From there, they were to run a pipe line up into the cave, using special plastic tubing which hooked together in a jiffy.

"Cover the piping with sand and gravel, so it won't be noticed," Tom added. "In the meantime, Bud and I will go to work on this setup here."

"Aye-aye, skipper!" Hank and Arv responded.

As they hurried out through the tunnel, Tom and Bud set to work with the tools they had brought along. The diesel was partly dismantled, sand poured into its fuel feed, and the generator windings ripped out. The boys then tore off and tangled all wiring leads to the electrical equipment, took apart much of the equipment itself, and smashed the control panel.

"Boy, if those Brungarian creeps get this setup working again, they're *really* geniuses!" Bud said as he and Tom paused a second.

"This is only the beginning, pal!" Tom said. "Let's tackle the machine!"

The huge earthquake device was a far more difficult proposition to disable. Its heavy structural parts had to be disassembled or pried apart, one by one. Both boys were streaked with sweat as they finished.

By this time, Hank and Arv had the piping installed halfway into the tunnel. Spurred on as if by a sixth sense of danger, Tom told them to go back to the beach and get the pump working while he and Bud connected the few remaining pipe lengths into the machine room.

Minutes later, their job done, Tom and Bud rushed out to the mouth of the cave and waved their flashlights. Soon the water could be heard boiling through the pipeline. It gushed out with a roar, flooding the machine room.

"Let's go!" Tom cried, yanking Bud's arm.

As they reached the beach and joined Hank and Arv, Tom's keen ears picked up the drone of a plane somewhere in the darkness.

He gave a yell of alarm and pointed skyward. A

ghostlike jet came zooming into view, boring straight toward them. All four broke into a mad dash for the seacopter.

They were halfway out on the reef when the plane leveled out of its dive with an earsplitting whine.

"Hide!" Tom shouted, fearing a bomb might be dropped.

All leaped for cover among the rocks. At the same instant, a fiery beam like a bolt of lightning shot from the plane. It seared th e spot on thereef they had just vacated!

"A ray gun!" Bud gasped.

The plane's speed had already carried it far past the island. Before it could maneuver around for another pass, Tom and his companions were on their feet, racing for the safety of the *Sea Hound*.

They were aboard and clamping shut the hatch lid as the jet made its second pass. This time its fiery ray glanced harmlessly off the seacopter's Tomasite sheathing. Seconds later, the *Sea Hound* had darted off beyond reach into the ocean waters.

"Whew! We really broke all speed records that time!" Arv panted.

The others looked at him with wan but triumphant grins. Then they began to speculate on what the beamlike bolt was, who was in the plane, and if their enemy knew who Tom's group were.

Dawn was streaking the sky when the seacopter arrived at Fearing Island. The adventurers flew back to Enterprises at once. Tom and Bud snatched a few hours' sleep in the apartment adjoining Tom's laboratory.

Later in the morning the whole group gathered in Tom's laboratory to recount the raid to Mr. Swift and Harlan Ames. A bell signal from the electronic brain brought them rushing to the decoder. Grim news awaited them. The message said:

> EXMAN TO SWIFTS. YOUR ENEMIES ARE NOW SURE I AM SPY. THEY PLAN TO DESTROY ME.

"No! It mustn't happen!" Tom cried in dismay. "Dad, I'll rescue him myself!"

His words were greeted with shocked protests from the others.

"Don't be crazy!" Bud said. "You wouldn't have a chance!"

"It would be suicide!" Arv Hanson declared.

Chow grabbed his young boss by the arm. "Brand my cayenne pepper, before I'd let you make a blame fool move like that, I'd rope an' hawg-tie you myself!"

Ames interjected the most convincing argument. "I know how you feel, Tom," he said sympathetically, "but I'm positive the United States government would never permit such a risky undertaking."

Tom was beside himself with anxiety. Not only had he worked and struggled to make the space brain's visit a scientific success, but also it was he who had thought of the scheme to use Exman as a spy. In Tom's eyes, if the Brungarian rebels were to destroy the brain's body, it would amount to murder! The young inventor knew that the destruction of the "body" would not destroy the energy, but that it would be "lost" as far as the earth was concerned.

Who knew, Tom asked himself, what priceless secrets the "brain" might ultimately yield to earth's scientific researchers? If the Brungarians were to succeed, this might deter the Swifts' space friends from ever attempting another visit to our planet!

In despair, Tom turned to his father. "You know how much is at stake, Dad!" he pleaded. "Isn't there something we can do?"

Mr. Swift had been silent, thoughtfully drumming his pencil on the workbench. He looked up.

"Tom, I can think of only one thing," he said. "Perhaps our friends on Planet X can help us. They said they would have no control over the energy until it was ready to return home. But maybe we can get them to help us transfer the energy back here - not by any means of earth transportation, but by some extraterrestrial means known to their scientists."

Tom's eyes kindled with hope. "Dad, that's a terrific idea!" he exclaimed. "Let's try!"

A message was quickly beamed out into space. Minutes went by. Then the machine signaled a reply.

It said:

WE WILL ATTEMPT RESCUE IF YOU WILL ARC A POWERFUL RADIO BEAM FROM POINT OF ORIGINAL EARTH LANDING TO POINT WHERE ENERGY IS NOW.

Moments later, a further message followed, giving technical instructions on how to project the beam. It ended:

NOTIFY US WHEN SETUP IS READY.

"Yahoo!" Chow whooped. "Brand my space guns, I reckon we'll get Ole Think Box home safe after all!"

"He's not home yet, Chow," Tom cautioned, grinning but still tense with worry. "Glad you said that, though. It reminds me that the first job on our hands is to build a new think box for Exman!"

With hope alive, Tom turned icy calm and buckled down to the work at hand. Before beginning construction of a new space robot, he contacted Exman via the electronic brain and asked him for his exact location in Brungaria. The answer came in precise latitude and longitude.

Next, Tom radioed instructions for the rescue plan. As soon as Exman was notified that the invisible force from Planet X was ready to transport his energy, he was to unlatch point five of his star head. He would then be free to attach his energy to the rescue beam and be arced back to the hillside spot near Enterprises, where Tom would have a new robot body waiting.

Exman replied tersely:

MESSAGE UNDERSTOOD. WILL COMPLY.

Tom snapped out orders. "Hank! Arv! Bud! And, Dad, we can sure use your help too! Every hour may be precious! We must construct a replica of Exman's robot container as fast as possible!"

Every resource of Swift Enterprises was convulsed into action. But for all their scientific miracles, the staff could not perform magic. The complicated robot device required hours of highly skilled construction.

Darkness had fallen by the time the energy container was ready. Meanwhile, a powerful transmitter and directional antenna had been set up at the hillside spot. Extensive reports on the condition of the ionosphere poured into headquarters.

The Swifts and their small group of trusted associates trucked the new robot and the electronic brain out to the site. Tom then signaled his space friends that he was ready. They responded with the exact time for the rescue attempt. Tom transmitted the information to Exman, who replied:

DANGER NEAR. BRUNGARIAN SCIENTISTS READY TO DESTROY ME.

"Great bellowin' buffaloes!" Chow gulped. "Please make it quick, Tom! We got to save that space critter!"

Tom glanced at his illuminated watch dial. The countdown ticked by. Suddenly his hand closed a switch, transmitting the rescue beam. More moments passed as the Swifts and the watchers strained their eyes toward the night sky.

"Here it comes!" Bud yelled suddenly.

A fiery bluish-white light had suddenly flamed into view. It grew steadily larger. Tom poised the container and opened one point of the star head.

Now the blue fireball was arcing down over the hillside, trailing its orange-red comet tail. It hissed into the container and Tom snapped shut the star head.

The next moment, the young inventor wavered and slumped unconscious!

CHAPTER XX

THE ROBOT SPY'S STORY

"Tom!" his father cried. Anxiously the others crowded around the lanky young inventor, who had fallen beside the new robot.

"Stand back! Give him air!" Bud urged. "How is he, Mr. Swift?"

The elder scientist was feeling Tom's wrist. "His pulse is beating, but it's a bit weak. He must have received a terrific shock from all that energy!... Tom!... Tom, son, can you hear me?"

The young inventor moaned and stirred faintly but his eyes did not open. His cheeks and lips seemed colorless in the glow of Mr. Swift's flashlight. Chow was terrified, hovering about helplessly.

"I'll call Doc Simpson to bring a pulmotor!" Hank exclaimed.

"Yes, do, Hank!" Mr. Swift pleaded. "Quick!"

An ambulance arrived a few minutes later. Doc Simpson and an attendant leaped out, and the resuscitation equipment - specially designed by the

Swifts for their plant infirmary - was hastily unloaded.

Anxious moments followed, but finally Tom began to respond to the treatment. Soon his eyes were open and he regained full consciousness. As Doc held a paper cup of water for him to sip, Tom smiled wanly.

"Okay." he murmured, "I'm all right now. Sorry if I scared you, Dad." He started to get up.

"It's a hospital bed for you, skipper. And no arguments!" Doc Simpson said sternly. "What happened here?"

"I believe," Mr. Swift answered, "that our space friends, in finding a way to move the energy back to us, had less close control over it on earth than when they sent it from space."

By midmorning the next day, Tom had awakened refreshed from a good night's sleep and felt normal again. Over Doc Simpson's protests, he insisted upon dressing and hurrying over to his laboratory.

Here he found his father working intently amid a jumble of mechanical parts, tools, and electronic equipment. Nearby stood Exman with a panel open in his upper body, exposing the controls and output equipment.

"Hi, Dad!" Tom exclaimed as he strode into the laboratory. "What's doing with Ole Think Box?"

Mr. Swift looked up with a smile of relief. "'Morning, son! All well again? That's wonderful! I'm just giving Exman an artificial speech mechanism. He's already briefed us via the electronic brain on the situation in Brungaria. But I thought it would be even better if he could tell us in person."

Details on the earthquake plot, Mr. Swift went on, had already been reported to the Defense Department. Tom's raid on Balala Island had effectively blocked further quake attempts.

The Brungarian rebels had become enraged by their failure to extract Exman's secrets, and had decided to disintegrate the robot creature and its brain energy. But the youthful Brungarian loyalist group had kept them so busy with resistance outbreaks that they had delayed too long.

"Lucky thing!" Tom put in with an affectionate grin at Exman. "If they had started to destroy him half an hour sooner, it might have been pretty sad for Ole Think Box!"

Tom was intrigued by his father's design for an artificial speech mechanism. After talking it over, they decided that Tom would go to work on a central computer device to integrate all the senses. He would also provide Exman with "ears," which would be sound-reception equipment. Mr. Swift, meanwhile, would continue work on the speech mechanism and also perfect the seeing equipment he had started earlier.

The day sped by as the two Swifts worked with feverish intensity. Lunch was eaten from their workbenches, but the inventors reluctantly halted at dinnertime.

After a tasty meal of fried chicken at home with Mrs. Swift and Sandy, both Toms returned to the plant. Father and son labored until well past midnight on their experiments. Then they snatched a few hours of sleep and resumed their tasks early the next morning.

By early afternoon an atmosphere of excitement pervaded Enterprises. The visitor from Planet X would soon be able to communicate directly with his earth friends! Bud, Chow, Hank Sterling, Arv Hanson, and Art Wiltessa gathered in the laboratory, along with several other Swift key men. Mrs. Swift, Sandy, and Phyl also arrived to watch.

At last the sensing equipment was completed and installed. Exman was ready to speak!

His voice came out haltingly, but as the words were selected from a vast taped collection, they were clear and bold:

GREETINGS TO YOU, MY EARTH FRIENDS!

Sandy gave a squeal of delight and the room echoed with applause for Exman's first effort. After a few adjustments, he was able to speak more freely and smoothly.

Tom whispered to Phyl, "Confidentially, we had a dummy run before lunchtime. At first, all Exman could do was croak like a frog."

Phyl, thrilled by the spectacle of a speaking space creature, gave the young inventor's hand a squeeze. "Tom, he's just wonderful!"

Tom agreed. "Our country owes him a lot for exposing the Brungarian rebel schemes."

To Tom's amazement, Exman's "ears" picked up his murmured words, even above the babble of the spectators crowding the room.

"Your country owes you much, Tom Swift," the creature said. "You conceived the idea of an electronic spy and found ways to block the rebels' destructive earthquake plans."

As Tom flushed at the crowd's applause, Exman continued, "Unless I am mistaken, you will soon learn that you have accomplished even more."

Tom was mystified by this. Meanwhile, the spectators listened spellbound as Exman went on talking, telling what he had learned of the valiant resistance efforts to overthrow the Brungarian rebels.

A short time later the telephone rang. Tom answered, and the operator informed him that John Thurston of Central Intelligence was calling.

"Great news, Tom," the CIA man said. "We've just learned that the rightful Brungarian government forces have struck hard in the capital city and at half a dozen other points. The rebel puppets and their troops have been crushed completely!"

Tom was enthusiastic over the news.

"That's not all," Thurston went on. "In case you don't realize it, the information which you supplied by means of your electronic spy is chiefly what enabled the government forces to win out. They've promised to dismantle the rebels' other two earthquake bases."

As Tom hung up and relayed the electrifying news, Bud and the others burst into cheers.

"It is all due to Tom Swift and his secret assistant," Exman said.

Tom was puzzled by the remark but had no time to ask what he meant as the people in the room crowded around to shake his hand. Mr. and Mrs. Swift smiled proudly at their son's latest triumph. Phyl and Sandy expressed their feelings by giving Tom a quick kiss.

"Hey! Where do I come in?" Bud protested.

Before the girls could answer, the door of the laboratory opened and Harlan Ames walked in, accompanied by a lean, gray-eyed young man with dark close-cropped hair. *Samson Narko!*

Chow let out a yelp of rage. "Why, brand my sagebrush hash, it's that double-crossin' Brungarian -"

"Hold it, Chow!" Ames cut short the outburst. "Allow me to introduce one of America's most effective counterespionage agents, Mr. Samson Narko!"

Tom and his friends were astounded. Narko himself smiled somewhat uncomfortably. "I can imagine how you all feel - you especially, Tom. But, believe me, I could not risk pulling my punches even when it put you all in grave peril, such as when I fired that missile across the bow of your sub. I could only hope that Tom Swift would succeed in eluding us."

Ames quickly briefed the others on Narko's background. Brungarian-born, he had received his engineering training in the United States and had learned to love America. When he saw his own country threatened by the forces of dictatorship, he had secretly offered his services to the CIA against the rebels. Soon afterward, the agency had approached him to become a counterspy.

"I dared not relax from my role as a spy for a moment," Narko added. "I even grabbed the chance to plant that cache of firearms in Latty's cellar to convince any rebel agents who might be watching me that I was on their side. Tom, the rebels gave me the job of hijacking your space robot. But, going on the brief messages that the CIA was able to get through to me, I guessed that you were using it as bait."

"I guess we all owe *you* an apology," Tom said. "And our thanks. We were lucky to have you on our side."

"He saved the lives of a number of loyalist prisoners and gave the government forces some vital tip-offs of his own," Ames added.

As Tom shook hands with Narko, the young Brungarian said warmly, "It is good to know that Tom Swift is my friend." With a chuckle, Narko added, "I know from experience that you certainly make a dangerous enemy!"

As the others gathered around to speak to Samson Narko and add their friendly congratulations, Bud slapped Tom on the back.

"Well, skipper, what's next on the schedule?"

For a moment Tom did not reply. He too wondered where his next scientific adventure would lead him.

Finally Tom turned to Bud. "I'm not sure. But who knows what space secrets Exman may have up his mechanical sleeve!"

*　*　*　*　*
*　*　*　*
*　*　*　*　*

[Errors noted by transcriber:

Tom and Bud wore swimming trunks under their slacks. *text reads* swimming Tom looked up, his blue eyes blazing. *text has period for comma* KIDNAPED! [chapter title] *and elsewhere spelling* "kidnaped" *consistent in text*]

Choose from Thousands of 1stWorldLibrary Classics By

A. M. Barnard
Ada Leverson
Adolphus William Ward
Aesop
Agatha Christie
Alexander Aaronsohn
Alexander Kielland
Alexandre Dumas
Alfred Gatty
Alfred Ollivant
Alice Duer Miller
Alice Turner Curtis
Alice Dunbar
Allen Chapman
Ambrose Bierce
Amelia E. Barr
Amory H. Bradford
Andrew Lang
Andrew McFarland Davis
Andy Adams
Anna Alice Chapin
Anna Sewell
Annie Besant
Annie Hamilton Donnell
Annie Payson Call
Annie Roe Carr
Annonaymous
Anton Chekhov
Arnold Bennett
Arthur Conan Doyle
Arthur M. Winfield
Arthur Ransome
Arthur Schnitzler
Atticus
B.H. Baden-Powell
B. M. Bower
B. C. Chatterjee
Baroness Emmuska Orczy
Baroness Orczy
Basil King
Bayard Taylor
Ben Macomber
Bertha Muzzy Bower
Bjornstjerne Bjornson
Booth Tarkington
Boyd Cable
Bram Stoker
C. Collodi
C. E. Orr

C. M. Ingleby
Carolyn Wells
Catherine Parr Traill
Charles A. Eastman
Charles Amory Beach
Charles Dickens
Charles Dudley Warner
Charles Farrar Browne
Charles Ives
Charles Kingsley
Charles Klein
Charles Hanson Towne
Charles Lathrop Pack
Charles Romyn Dake
Charles Whibley
Charles Willing Beale
Charlotte M. Braeme
Charlotte M. Yonge
Charlotte Perkins Stetson
Clair W. Hayes
Clarence Day Jr.
Clarence E. Mulford
Clemence Housman
Confucius
Coningsby Dawson
Cornelis DeWitt Wilcox
Cyril Burleigh
D. H. Lawrence
Daniel Defoe
David Garnett
Dinah Craik
Don Carlos Janes
Donald Keyhoe
Dorothy Kilner
Dougan Clark
Douglas Fairbanks
E. Nesbit
E.P.Roe
E. Phillips Oppenheim
Earl Barnes
Edgar Rice Burroughs
Edith Van Dyne
Edith Wharton
Edward Everett Hale
Edward J. O'Biren
Edward S. Ellis
Edwin L. Arnold
Eleanor Atkins
Eliot Gregory

Elizabeth Gaskell
Elizabeth McCracken
Elizabeth Von Arnim
Ellem Key
Emerson Hough
Emilie F. Carlen
Emily Dickinson
Enid Bagnold
Enilor Macartney Lane
Erasmus W. Jones
Ernie Howard Pie
Ethel May Dell
Ethel Turner
Ethel Watts Mumford
Eugenie Foa
Eugene Wood
Eustace Hale Ball
Evelyn Everett-green
Everard Cotes
F. H. Cheley
F. J. Cross
F. Marion Crawford
Federick Austin Ogg
Ferdinand Ossendowski
Francis Bacon
Francis Darwin
Frances Hodgson Burnett
Frances Parkinson Keyes
Frank Gee Patchin
Frank Harris
Frank Jewett Mather
Frank L. Packard
Frank V. Webster
Frederic Stewart Isham
Frederick Trevor Hill
Frederick Winslow Taylor
Friedrich Kerst
Friedrich Nietzsche
Fyodor Dostoyevsky
G.A. Henty
G.K. Chesterton
Gabrielle E. Jackson
Garrett P. Serviss
Gaston Leroux
George A. Warren
George Ade
Geroge Bernard Shaw
George Durston
George Ebers

George Eliot
George Gissing
George MacDonald
George Meredith
George Orwell
George Sylvester Viereck
George Tucker
George W. Cable
George Wharton James
Gertrude Atherton
Gordon Casserly
Grace E. King
Grace Gallatin
Grace Greenwood
Grant Allen
Guillermo A. Sherwell
Gulielma Zollinger
Gustav Flaubert
H. A. Cody
H. B. Irving
H.C. Bailey
H. G. Wells
H. H. Munro
H. Irving Hancock
H. Rider Haggard
H. W. C. Davis
Haldeman Julius
Hall Caine
Hamilton Wright Mabie
Hans Christian Andersen
Harold Avery
Harold McGrath
Harriet Beecher Stowe
Harry Castlemon
Harry Coghill
Harry Houidini
Hayden Carruth
Helent Hunt Jackson
Helen Nicolay
Hendrik Conscience
Hendy David Thoreau
Henri Barbusse
Henrik Ibsen
Henry Adams
Henry Ford
Henry Frost
Henry James
Henry Jones Ford
Henry Seton Merriman
Henry W Longfellow
Herbert A. Giles

Herbert Carter
Herbert N. Casson
Herman Hesse
Hildegard G. Frey
Homer
Honore De Balzac
Horace B. Day
Horace Walpole
Horatio Alger Jr.
Howard Pyle
Howard R. Garis
Hugh Lofting
Hugh Walpole
Humphry Ward
Ian Maclaren
Inez Haynes Gillmore
Irving Bacheller
Isabel Hornibrook
Israel Abrahams
Ivan Turgenev
J.G.Austin
J. Henri Fabre
J. M. Barrie
J. Macdonald Oxley
J. S. Fletcher
J. S. Knowles
J. Storer Clouston
Jack London
Jacob Abbott
James Allen
James Andrews
James Baldwin
James Branch Cabell
James DeMille
James Joyce
James Lane Allen
James Lane Allen
James Oliver Curwood
James Oppenheim
James Otis
James R. Driscoll
Jane Austen
Jane L. Stewart
Janet Aldridge
Jens Peter Jacobsen
Jerome K. Jerome
John Burroughs
John Cournos
John F. Kennedy
John Gay
John Glasworthy

John Habberton
John Joy Bell
John Kendrick Bangs
John Milton
John Philip Sousa
Jonas Lauritz Idemil Lie
Jonathan Swift
Joseph A. Altsheler
Joseph Carey
Joseph Conrad
Joseph E. Badger Jr
Joseph Hergesheimer
Joseph Jacobs
Jules Vernes
Julian Hawthrone
Julie A Lippmann
Justin Huntly McCarthy
Kakuzo Okakura
Kenneth Grahame
Kenneth McGaffey
Kate Langley Bosher
Kate Langley Bosher
Katherine Cecil Thurston
Katherine Stokes
L. A. Abbot
L. T. Meade
L. Frank Baum
Latta Griswold
Laura Dent Crane
Laura Lee Hope
Laurence Housman
Lawrence Beasley
Leo Tolstoy
Leonid Andreyev
Lewis Carroll
Lewis Sperry Chafer
Lilian Bell
Lloyd Osbourne
Louis Hughes
. Louis Tracy
Louisa May Alcott
Lucy Fitch Perkins
Lucy Maud Montgomery
Luther Benson
Lydia Miller Middleton
Lyndon Orr
M. Corvus
M. H. Adams
Margaret E. Sangster
Margret Howth
Margaret Vandercook

Margret Penrose
Maria Edgeworth
Maria Thompson Daviess
Mariano Azuela
Marion Polk Angellotti
Mark Overton
Mark Twain
Mary Austin
Mary Catherine Crowley
Mary Cole
Mary Hastings Bradley
Mary Roberts Rinehart
Mary Rowlandson
M. Wollstonecraft Shelley
Maud Lindsay
Max Beerbohm
Myra Kelly
Nathaniel Hawthrone
Nicolo Machiavelli
O. F. Walton
Oscar Wilde
Owen Johnson
P.G. Wodehouse
Paul and Mabel Thorne
Paul G. Tomlinson
Paul Severing
Percy Brebner
Peter B. Kyne
Plato
R. Derby Holmes
R. L. Stevenson
R. S. Ball
Rabindranath Tagore
Rahul Alvares
Ralph Bonehill
Ralph Henry Barbour
Ralph Victor
Ralph Waldo Emmerson
Rene Descartes
Rex Beach

Rex E. Beach
Richard Harding Davis
Richard Jefferies
Richard Le Gallienne
Robert Barr
Robert Frost
Robert Gordon Anderson
Robert L. Drake
Robert Lansing
Robert Lynd
Robert Michael Ballantyne
Robert W. Chambers
Rosa Nouchette Carey
Rudyard Kipling
Samuel B. Allison
Samuel Hopkins Adams
Sarah Bernhardt
Sarah C. Hallowell
Selma Lagerlof
Sherwood Anderson
Sigmund Freud
Standish O'Grady
Stanley Weyman
Stella Benson
Stella M. Francis
Stephen Crane
Stewart Edward White
Stijn Streuvels
Swami Abhedananda
Swami Parmananda
T. S. Ackland
T. S. Arthur
The Princess Der Ling
Thomas A. Janvier
Thomas A Kempis
Thomas Anderton
Thomas Bailey Aldrich
Thomas Bulfinch
Thomas De Quincey
Thomas Dixon

Thomas H. Huxley
Thomas Hardy
Thomas More
Thornton W. Burgess
U. S. Grant
Valentine Williams
Various Authors
Vaughan Kester
Victor Appleton
Victoria Cross
Virginia Woolf
Wadsworth Camp
Walter Camp
Walter Scott
Washington Irving
Wilbur Lawton
Wilkie Collins
Willa Cather
Willard F. Baker
William Dean Howells
William le Queux
W. Makepeace Thackeray
William W. Walter
William Shakespeare
Winston Churchill
Yei Theodora Ozaki
Yogi Ramacharaka
Young E. Allison
Zane Grey